Sebastian Dümling, Zhenwei Wang (eds.)
Being There, but How?

Sociology

Sebastian Dümling (PD Dr.) is a cultural anthropologist and historian. He works as a Lecturer at the Chair of European Ethnology/Empirical Cultural Studies at the University of Würzburg (Germany) and is affiliated as a Privatdozent at the Faculty of Philosophy at the University of Basel (Switzerland).

Zhenwei Wang is a PhD candidate in sociology and a member of the Institute for World Society Studies at Bielefeld University (Germany). Her research interests include migration, gender, aging and family transition in China and in East Asia. Her PhD dissertation investigates translocal kinning and caregiving practices in contemporary China.

Sebastian Dümling, Zhenwei Wang (eds.)

Being There, but How?

On the Transformation of Presence
in (Post-)Pandemic Times

[transcript]

Funded by
Bielefeld University
Deutsche Forschungsgemeinschaft (DFG)
Seminar of Cultural Studies/European Ethnology at the University of Basel

Bibliographic information published by the Deutsche Nationalbibliothek
The Deutsche Nationalbibliothek lists this publication in the Deutsche Nationalbibliografie; detailed bibliographic data are available in the Internet at https://dnb.dnb.de/

First published in 2024 by transcript Verlag, Bielefeld
© Sebastian Dümling, Zhenwei Wang (eds.)

Cover layout: Maria Arndt, Bielefeld
Cover illustration: ElConsigliere / AdobeStock
Proofread: Philip Saunders (saundersproof@hotmail.com)
Printed by: Majuskel Medienproduktion GmbH, Wetzlar
https://doi.org/10.14361/9783839468807
Print-ISBN: 978-3-8376-6880-3
PDF-ISBN: 978-3-8394-6880-7
ISSN of series: 2703-1691
eISSN of series: 2747-3007

Contents

Preface 7

Authors 9

On the Transformation of Presences – An Introduction
Sebastian Dümling 11

Scoping the Virtual World. Identity Reshaping as an Epistemological Prerequisite
for Research
Gabriel Stoiciu 19

Doing Presence. On the Construction of Relations and Realities in Online
Teaching Settings
Marion Näser-Lather 39

Riding Tools and Spiritual Excursion: Modes of Human Presence and Tool Usage
Jung Yeon Kim 57

Virtual and Physical Ways of Being Present in Odissi Dance Networks in
Bhubaneswar in India
Barbara Čurda 83

Forced and Uncertain Co-presence. Smart Cameras and Distant Homework
Supervision in Eastern China
Zhenwei Wang.. 111

The Class Diary of the Pandemic. Comics of the Transformations of the 'Presence'
in Brazilian Schools during the COVID-19 Pandemic
João Pedro Rangel Gomes da Silva and Matheus Fred Schulze 131

Preface

This anthology is based on a panel organised by Eberhard Wolff and Sebastian Düm-ling at the 17th Biennial of the European Association of Social Anthropologists in Belfast in 2022. We, the editors, would like to thank Eberhard Wolff very much for co-organising this panel!

We would also like to thank all the speakers, especially those who took the trouble to adapt their papers for this volume.

The publication of this book would not have been possible without the generous support of our funding partners:

We would like to thank the Open Access Publication Fund of Bielefeld University and the German Research Foundation (DFG) for supporting the publication costs. We would also like to thank the Department of Cultural Studies and European Eth-nology at the University of Basel for its generous support.

Zhenwei Wang (Bielefeld) and Sebastian Dümling (Würzburg/Basel)

Authors

Dr. Sebastian Dümling is a cultural anthropologist and historian. He works as a Senior Lecturer at the Chair of European Ethnology/Empirical Cultural Studies at the University of Würzburg (Germany) and is affiliated as a Privatdozent at the Faculty of Philosophy at the University of Basel (Switzerland).

Dr. Gabriel Stoiciu is Senior Researcher at Francisc Rainer Institute of Anthropology of Romanian Academy and holds a Phd in Philosophy at University of Bucharest (Romania). His academic background relies on fieldwork carried out in Romania and France.

Dr. Marion Näser-Lather is a cultural anthropologist. She works as an Assistant Professor at the Institute for History and European Ethnology at the University of Innsbruck (Austria) and is affiliated as a Privatdozent at the Faculty of Social Sciences and Philosophy at the University of Marburg (Germany).

Jung Yeon Kim is a multimedia artist pursuing in parallel anthropological research to nourish both her plastic works and their theoretical foundation. On completing BA in Fine Art and Art Science at Hongik University (South Korea) and MA in Contemporary Art at University of Paris 8, she undertook doctoral research in Anthropology at the École des hautes études en sciences sociales (EHESS, France).

Dr. Barbara Čurda is a Marie Curie fellow and anthropologist. She is presently working under the Université Clermont Auvergne (UCA, France) and with affiliation to the French Institute of Pondicherry (IFP, India), on the project GATRODI – Gender asymmetry in the transmission of Odissi dance in India – a case study.

Zhenwei Wang is a Ph.D. candidate in sociology at Bielefeld University (Germany), specializing in migration, gender, digitalization, and family transitions in China and East Asia. Her chapter in this volume earned her the H. Russell Bernard Graduate Student Travel Award at the Society for Anthropological Sciences Spring Meeting in 2023.

João Pedro Rangel Gomes da Silva is a social anthropologist and social scientist. He has a master's degree in social Anthropology from the Universidade Estadual de Campinas (Brazil). Currently, he is a M.A./Ph.D. student in the Italian Studies program at UC Berkeley (United States).

Matheus Fred Schulze is a sociologist at the State University of Campinas (Brazil). He is currently studying Design at the British School of Creative Arts and Technology (United Kingdom).

On the Transformation of Presences – An Introduction

Sebastian Dümling

Presence – empirical fractions

Between 2020 and 2021, two cohorts of students at the University of Basel – similar to probably most universities worldwide – began their studies under COVID-19 conditions. Accordingly, they got to know the university, attended the courses, and engaged in conversations with fellow students and lecturers exclusively in a mediated form via platforms such as Zoom or Teams. This led to a strange effect for me as a lecturer and especially as a student advisor.

During the fully mediated semesters, I had countless advising talks with students via Zoom that were far more personal, emotional and, thus, intimate than similar conversations in direct face-to-face communication in my office. Students sitting in their teenage bedrooms in their parents' home have told me frequently, sometimes in tears, how dissatisfied they were with their Zoom studies in mediated COVID times and how "damn depressing" the whole situation was for them. I gained insights into the students' room dispositions as well as their emotional arrangements that had previously been far removed from me. After a few sessions, I knew their stuffed animals, which pop stars' posters hung on their walls and whether they liked or disliked tidying their desks. Thus, this communicative shift created an unusual figuration of intimacy, an arrangement of closeness consisting of actors, media (devices), feelings, spaces and objects. Strangely enough, distance teaching led to less distanced communication.

When the university reopened, I met the students with whom I had previously entered such intimate figurations, and we continued the counselling sessions in my office. However, now, in what should have been a face-to-face communication, we experienced a breaching of the familiar relationships we had built during our former Zoom sessions: At the same moment, we were simultaneously strangers to each other as much as we were familiar. However we – the consultant and the student – had no social script at our disposal for dealing with this strange familiarity. We had to learn that the different modes of our presence – our appearance in the video call and in my office – each afford unique selves and, thus, distinctive communicative pairings: Without media – whether as "body glossings" in Goffman's sense (1971, 27) or as apparatuses of representation – we would not be able to communicate externally what we suspect inside ourselves. In this way, we experienced impressively and emotionally how we were aligned with the media settings through which each of our selves encountered other people's selves (Ronzhyn and Cardenal 2023).

In other words, these two settings create two different "cultures of presence" (Gumbrecht 2004). Remarkably, the mediatized culture enables a deeper dimension of intimacy here because, I assume, it increases visual proximity and, at the same time, restricts sensuality: Ego sees Alter – and its world of things – in closest proximity, but without having to process the highly contingent physical-haptic dimension of this perception. This condition makes it easier to be close while, simultaneously, being a stranger. This argument goes hand in hand with a basic assumption about physical presence formulated classically by Erwin Goffman (1959): Bodies that are present challenge us communicatively because we sense that their territoriality goes beyond the mere cover of the skin. However, we cannot ask the other body exactly what its territoriality is. If it were not so embarrassing, we probably could ask the other person who inhabits the other body. Nevertheless, if we were to do this, we would no longer be having an everyday conversation but an intimate one, for which new, more complicated scripts were necessary.

The disruptions I experienced as a student counsellor had consequences for my teaching, or more precisely, for my teaching of theoretical concepts. It came as a surprise that students could now understand some specific theoretical debates in the social sciences quite well due to their pandemic media experiences. In my discipline, cultural anthropology, this applies above all to the theoretical discussions surrounding the so-called 'crisis of representation'.[1] While it has always been a vast didactic challenge for me to convey the methodological and epistemological consequences of the writing-culture debate from the 1980s to young students, this no longer seemed so complicated. The core of this debate became a very empirical everyday experience for many students in COVID-19 times.

Without formulating this conceptually, many students have learnt implicitly that there is a constitutive relationship between media environment and living environment, between media *Umwelt* and *Lebenswelt*. They have experienced that the inherent logic of media systems determines, to a certain degree, what these systems observe. The students have experienced interactions being thrown back on the discursive and technical conditions of the media which make life and interactions communicable. This seemingly pretty abstract idea now reflected an everyday experience that could be easily conveyed. At the same time, however, I realized that the theoretical considerations about everyday life I teach in courses now seemed very fractured.

---

1   A brief reminder of what this debate was about: It was about nothing less than the uncertainty if the ethnographic account does not primarily say something about the form of the ethnographic account or about what is ethnographically observed.

If everyday life changes, does not the theory of everyday life also have to be new and different?

Presence - theoretical fractures

From a classical phenomenological perspective, everyday life is the territory of reality where basic interactions occur between at least two individuals present. Two actors encounter each other as black boxes and must somehow reduce the contingency of doable actions so that communication is possible. These individuals are physically present at a shared location, observe each other's body and consider the physical presence of the other in their actions. This spatial-temporal co-presence situation implies challenges and resources for mutual coordination. Everydayness is given when these interactions are processed according to tacit knowledge, whereby the selection of interactional steps is not reflected consciously but made implicitly (Goffman 1959). Integrating digital communication into everyday life has disrupted such a theory of everyday life. Finally, all the grand theories of everyday life agree to focus on face-to-face communication among people who are physically present, whether Alfred Schütz's "Lebenswelt", Erwin Goffman's interactionism, or the communicative practices to which Harold Garfinkel and Harvey Sacks have turned.

According to such conceptions, the actors draw on enculturated scripts, bodies of knowledge, format templates and role expectations, so that expectable practices can follow. Thus, everyday life is the area of physically perceived reality in which actors refer to incorporated macrostructural scripts and schemes. Without this reference, it would be precarious and problematic. Referring to Husserl's famous metaphor, everyday life can be seen as the realm of the world in which actors can drift as if in a stream without having to leave the stream: the stream of never-to-be-explained actions and assertions (2009, 162 ff.). This everydayness characterizes precisely those interactions between present bodies that lie below the perception threshold of conscious interaction. Goffman calls such everyday interactions "encounters" (1961), whereas Niklas Luhmann uses the witty expression of the "Kommunikation au trottoir" (1986, 75): According to Luhmann, it is a paradigmatic scene of everyday life that we walk along the sidewalk and rush past other people without having to address them as interaction partners. They are strangers with whom we have wordlessly agreed to remain strangers – without this agreement leading to closeness. Accordingly, one can ask if a Zoom-like everyday life is possible at all, since there are no sidewalks in Zoom where unintentional interactions could occur.[2]

---

2   Therefore, it is not surprising that journalistic articles have also focused on the lack of "Zufallsbegegnungen" (encounters by chance) in virtual spaces and asked how elementary

Karin Knorr-Cetina (2009) coined the term "response presence" to mark the co-temporality of communication participants, meaning that they can react to each other without any temporal delay in the same physical environment. According to this, the shared perception of the physical environment provides the framework for the interactive experience of presence. In addition, there are the requisites, the props, the culturally labelled and marking objects, which denote a specific presence as common reference points precisely when they are in the background of the everyday stage. Following this argument, Luhmann (2002, 102–111) points out laconically that it needs the presence of specific tables and chairs for young people to call each other students.

Moreover, the argument has even been put forward that interactive attendance systems are, to a certain extent, decoupled from social systems (Kieserling 1999, 25f.): The intrinsically organized patterns of the interaction would eventually predominate social markers in their formative power for the act. Finally, in an interaction, (at least) two bodies would have to arrange themselves in such a way as to form a temporally bound unit, but without forgetting that they are autonomous units. To a certain extent, this is the productive paradox of every interaction: Without bodies, interaction is impossible, but without interaction, the individual body cannot be perceived in its individuality.

These phenomenological, theoretical figures, having emerged during the 20th century, certainly did not foresee that in the 21st century, a certain part of this everyday interaction occurs between bodies which are physically distant. In this respect, empirical studies that build on this theoretical tradition must always insert the phrase that the concept of interaction used by those such as Schütz, Goffman and Garfinkel exclusively describes physically present people and must be adapted to digital time. The extent to which digital presences have become everyday life in just a few years can be seen in the fact that an empirically and theoretically impressively dense study from 2015 which deals with videoconferencing in ethnomethodological terms starts from the premise that videoconferencing is not everyday life but a break in everyday life (Mondada 2015).

What I would like to stress here is that the social sciences are still waiting for a grand theory of digital everyday life – a theory conceptualizing everyday interactions regarding digital and physical presences. There are certainly numerous reformulations and extensions of theories of everyday life. But there is still no genuinely new theory that is explicitly dedicated to our hybrid everyday life.

---

such encounters are, for example, for everyday office life. Cf. https://www.faz.net/aktuell/kar
riere-hochschule/kolumne-nine-to-five-auf-dem-virtuellen-flur-19403474.html (24 January
2024).

The contributions to this anthology certainly do not attempt to provide such a theory. Instead, they are empirical explorations of everyday life in which presence between those present can become precarious.

Presence – empirical observations, conceptual reflections

The contributions in this anthology are based on a panel that I (co-)chaired with Eberhard Wolff (Zurich) at the EASA Congress 2022 in Belfast.[3] We had initially planned only to discuss the new COVID-related everyday media life on the panel. But among the submissions were excellent contributions that went beyond COVID, which sharpened our perspectives on the mediated university.

This combination made us realize that COVID was ultimately just a catalyst for a change that would have happened even without the Zoom semesters. Nevertheless, students were particularly affected by the "zoomification" of the university and, thus, the mediatization of everyday life. That is why it was important for us to invite not only senior researchers as contributors, but also the voices of (post) graduate students.

Accordingly, this anthology gathers contributions written by both junior and senior researchers, master students as well as professors. I am also pleased that the contributors and their fields refer to three continents: America (Brazil), Asia (China, India, South Korea) and Europe (Austria, Germany, Romania). This allows the volume to capture a wide range of experiences and empirical observations. Therefore, the aim is not to find a conclusive answer to the question of how everyday media can be conceptualized. Rather, the aim is to compile a broad panorama of observations, theoretical considerations or even just thought experiments of how different forms of presence are organized together and alongside each other.

The first contribution "Scoping the virtual world. Identity reshaping as an epistemological prerequisite for research" delves into the impact of virtual reality on identity creation and self-expression. It emphasizes the need for social scientists to conduct phenomenological analysis before virtual fieldwork, raising questions about data validity in this unique environment. Gabriel Stoiciu suggests using an 'a priori' intellectual lens to navigate potential distortions, incorporating both 'etic' and 'emic' perspectives.

In "Doing Presence. On the construction of relations and realities in online teaching settings", Marion Näser-Lather investigates digital co-presence in online university teaching during the COVID-19 pandemic. Drawing from an interdisciplinary perspective, the author combines media theory, sociology, phenomenology

---

3   I thank Eberhard Wolff very much for the co-organization of the panel—and for the great time we spent together in Belfast!

and actor-network theory, using personal observations, surveys at German universities and statements from academics.

Jung Yeon Kim examines how tools, both ancient ritual objects and modern Virtual Reality (VR) tools, expand our understanding of immaterial worlds in her article "Riding tools and spiritual excursion. Modes of human presence and tool usage". These tools serve as symbolic indicators, which transport the mind and body to new realms, shaping diverse belief systems and accommodating the post-human presence in our conceptual world map.

Barbara Čurda reflects on the concept of presence amid the COVID-19 pandemic, exploring differences in "Virtual and physical ways of being present in Odissi dance networks in Bhubaneswar in India". Drawing on her fieldwork in Bhubaneswar, India, she focuses on Odissi dance activity, emphasizing how pandemic constraints altered physical contact and highlighting the relational nature of presence within a network of entities.

The article "Forced and uncertain co-presence. Smart cameras and distant homework supervision in Eastern China" explores technology-mediated distant homework supervision in that part of China. Based on her fieldwork, Zhenwei Wang analyses the use of smart cameras by migrant parents, and reveals that the technology creates a sense of 'forced co-presence' and 'uncertain co-presence' for the children while closely monitoring their homework.

The anthology concludes with the paper "The Class Diary of the pandemic. Comics of the transformations of the 'presence' in Brazilian schools during the COVID-19 pandemic" by João Pedro Rangel Gomes da Silva and Matheus Fred Schulze. They deal with an anthropological diary, i.e. "the Class Diary" which captured the diverse experiences of a new sense of 'presence' during the pandemic, blending fear of the present with hope for future change. The study specifically examined transformations in online teacher-student relationships, resulting in a distinctive virtual and everyday 'presence'. In order to convey these experiences artistically, the Class Diary was transformed into a comic book, representing diverse perspectives amid the uncertainties of the pandemic.

Bibliography

Goffman, Erwin. 1959. The Presentation of Self in Everyday Life. Garden City, NY: Anchor Books.
–––. 1961. Encounters: Two Studies in the Sociology of Interaction. Indianapolis: Bobbs-Merrill.
–––. 1971. Relations in Public. Microstudies of the Public Order. New York: Harper & Row.

Gumbrecht, Hans Ulrich. 2004. Production of Presence: What Meaning Cannot Convey, Redwood City: Stanford University Press.

Husserl, Edmund. 2009. Ideen zu einer reinen Phänomenologie und phänomenologischen Philosophie. Hamburg: Meiner.

Kieserling, André. 1999. Kommunikation unter Anwesenden. Studien über Interaktionssysteme. Frankfurt am Main: Suhrkamp.

Knorr-Cetina, Karin. 2009. "The Synthetic Situation: Interactionism for a Global World." Symbolic Interaction 32: 61–87.

Luhmann, Niklas. 1986. Ökologische Kommunikation: Kann die moderne Gesellschaft sich auf Ökologische Gefährdungen einstellen? Opladen: Westdeutscher Verlag.

–––. 2002. Das Erziehungssystem der Gesellschaft. Frankfurt am Main: Suhrkamp.

Mondada, Lorenza. 2015. "Ouverture et préouverture des réunions visiophoniques." Réseaux, 6/194: 39–84.

Ronzhyn, Alexander, and Ana Sofia Cardenal. 2023. "Defining Affordances in Social Media Research: A Literature Review." New Media & Society 25: 3165–3188.

Scoping the Virtual World. Identity Reshaping as an Epistemological Prerequisite for Research

Gabriel Stoiciu

Abstract *The experience of 'being in' the virtual world facilitates the creation of new 'personae' or just enables the innermost uninhibited 'presence' of an individual. Once inside this cultural environment, a social scientist has to engage in a phenomenological endeavour over the individual and social impact of the Internet, before tackling the actual fieldwork. Becoming a part of virtual reality offers the opportunity of reconsidering one's own identity and, furthermore, of exploring the various identities of other individuals who are more or less familiar to us in the real world.*

This challenging epistemological environment raises a self-implied questioning of the validity of data gathered here. Each virtual community is a creator and a promoter of its own cyber-culture, more or less linked to existing traits in the real world. An additional instrument seems useful, if not necessary, to grasp the ethnographic quality of fieldwork in the virtual world better: an 'a priori' intellectual lens capable of helping the researcher in social sciences to anticipate and manage the possible diversions that the virtual environment could inflict on the collection and, ultimately, on the validity of data. This instrument, both 'etic' and 'emic', should comprise a body of inquiries that lead to a self-questioning about the congruence of means and intentions of the researcher, while recording and sharing various experiences in the cyberspace of today and the metaverse of tomorrow. This approach should also consider an appraisal of the extent to which the evolutionary trends of cyberspace and metaverse – designed by private multinational agents – might preserve the cultural complexity of the human being apart from its status as mere 'user' of digital platforms.

Keywords *cyberspace; social phenomenology; telepresence; virtual reality; digital anthropology*

Introduction: The long journey of *Cyberspace* into *Metaverse*

Who is to say that an artificial intelligence (AI) linked to a three-dimensional printer could not create, in a foreseeable future, its own physical world? It could just as easily negotiate a salary for its services, open a bank account and make some smart investments, pay its taxes and utilities, buy a piece of property and, ultimately, start nesting. Till then, people and machines have plenty of opportunities to get to know each other better while navigating cyberspace or exploring virtual environments, laying byte by byte the shapes and colours of the metaverse.

The internet represents, in advanced societies, an omnipresent and omniscient tool, which gradually, in association with AI expressions such as Chat GPT, seems to also be gaining omnipotence. An individual in front of a computer, a tablet or a smartphone engaged in a conversation with another is actually participating in a dialogue of four. Electronic devices, by means of their software, often leave their own fingerprint on the communication process – examples are the annoying mishaps the autocomplete software can instil in text messages. All of this is amplified considerably when dozens of people are able to simultaneously join the same conversation. However, this prospective cultural change – through the impact of dazzling advances in digital technologies – might give hope that our online presence could improve the real world into an – 'upgraded' – more empathic society as a whole. Acting in this non-physical space opens the way to the possibility of reconstructing oneself while exploring the identity of other people.

The ever-expanding world of connected groups and individuals relying on a myriad of simultaneous exchanges of information via the internet is generally referred to as 'cyberspace' or, in a broader sense, the 'virtual world'. A person must obtain a digital identity and, according to one's needs, join a virtual community to gain access to this 'man-made universe'. From a technical point of view, the virtual identity encompasses a unique and complex digital marker given by the device itself (media access control code or International Mobile Equipment Identity), the address of the internet service provider (Internet Protocol), a username and, accordingly, a profile – required in order to access some specific web services or integrate a social network.

Social Media has the potential to become a major source of information and entertainment for anybody who owns a computer, a tablet or a smartphone and can use the Internet. Cyberspace represents an ideal environment for displaying the most hidden or unexplored resources or features of someone's personality (which, as it stands, are not always positive). Or, it may unleash a ludic impulse to fashion random characters just for the sake of it. The anonymity and the possibility of creating several personal profiles might also contribute – like in a process of phenomenological reduction – to the intuition and/or expression of a more intimate identity, of the core essence of an individual – apart from everyday conveniences and constraints. Therefore, online environments offer social scientists the possibility of grasping and analysing new forms of sociability facilitated by digital interaction. Furthermore, this medium provides new challenges for reconsidering even the most profound apprehension of intersubjectivity.

This chapter addresses the change into perspective brought to anthropology by immersion into the virtual world. Emerging from the metaphysical and philosophical approaches to the ontology of humankind, anthropology strives to put forward scientific knowledge about the specific traits of a particular community. It is a discipline which emphasizes the epistemological gain brought by a researcher's subjective trained perspective. However, in the case of new communities developed through digital networked technologies, the classic academic training for ethnographic fieldwork seems insufficient, if not inadequate. The virtualization of more and more human activities (from medicine and various manufacturing industries to client services and even politics) raises a major challenge for the epistemological relevance of classic ethnographic fieldwork. For now, a hybrid approach (integrating a virtual community and also having face-to-face encounters with at least some of its members) remains fruitful. However, the progress of the metaverse will, for all means and purposes, lead to a massive migration of social scientists to the virtual dominion.

Scoping the virtual world, experiencing this new intersubjectivity realm, implies having to unequivocally submit oneself to an identity reshaping process. In this digital environment, the relationship Ego-Alter comes inherently through the mediation of electronic devices whose technological bias cannot be overlooked. This cyber-symbiosis has the potential of inducing a circumstantial reification of the interlocutor value system, hence, a fundamental lack of trust. An a priori phenomenological perspective on 'being' in the virtual world has the potential of leading an anthropologist to perform an authentic epistemological itinerary on cultural outcomes of virtual communities.

Being there ... a virtual presence is all you need

Presence in a collective digital environment (e.g. social media platform or online virtual reality networked software)[1] requires an epistemological challenge for an anthropologist, which can only be tackled from a phenomenological perspective. The return into the non-virtual world – necessary in order to proceed to a comparative analysis – implies a forthwith auto-reflexive search of the feeling of 'being there' and, consequently, of the possible bias induced by the particularities of the technological equipment which ensures the mediation or even the immersion.

---

1   In this work, I have employed the 'virtual world' in the broad sense of any digital environment ranging from the first Advanced Research Projects Agency Network connection to the most advanced and integrative evolution of the metaverse. I refer to virtual reality only in the case of simulated digital environments (such as Counter-Strike, Second Life or Mesh) with professional or entertaining purposes.

Jonathan Steuer (1992) states that presence implies that focus is given to the mediated environment rather than to the immediate physical environment. The term refers "to the perception of those surroundings" (Steuer 1992, 5). In other words, the cognitive system is invested in the digital universe to the point where it is captured in an "illusion of nonmediation" which can only occur concomitantly with the media user's willingness to suspend disbelief and their knowledge of prior experience with the medium (Lombard and Ditton 2006). "An 'illusion of nonmediation' occurs when a person fails to perceive or acknowledge the existence of a medium in his/her communication environment and responds as he/she would if the medium were not there" (Lombard and Ditton 2006).

In this relation with the virtual world, the term employed currently by social scientists for conceptual clarification reasons is 'telepresence' as promoted by Marvin Minsky (1980). Telepresence implies a sense of being in a mediated environment (Draper et al. 1998), sensing the other during a mediatized communication (Bracken and Skalski 2010) or just being in a machine-generated world: the "sense of being physically present with virtual object(s) at the remote teleoperator site" (Sheridan 1992). Sheridan returns to the term 'presence' for the larger virtual space (the totality of mediated experience) – which could comprise "three variables: the extent of sensory information, control of relation of sensors to environment, and the ability to modify the physical environment" (Sheridan 1992, 4). As digital media use increases, it provides an increasing feeling of "social presence" (Westerman and Skalski 2010).

While acting in the virtual world, an individual can instantaneously connect and have a belonging experience to groups larger than ever possible with human physical abilities. Zhao introduce the term 'telecopresence' for the situation when people are able to "share a community of time without sharing a community of physical space" (2015, 114). He explains that in telecopresence, "individuals are physically remote from one another, hence 'tele'; but in the sense that they are able to reach one another in real or near-real time through electronic mediation, the individuals are temporally together with one another, hence 'copresence'" (Zhao 2015, 115). Mediated immediacy is understood to be a continuation of the mediatedness of the physical/lived body's experience of its environment (Lindmann and Schunemann 2020).

David Chalmers defines virtual reality as immersive, generating "perceptual experience of the environment from a perspective within it, giving the user the sense of 'presence': that is, the sense of really being present at that perspective" (2017, 312). This view is completed by Slater and Wilbur (1997), who make a clear distinction by ascribing the term 'immersive' to technology and 'presence' to a user's subjective experience. Immersion describes the extent to which the computer displays are capable of delivering an inclusive, extensive, surrounding and vivid illusion of reality to the senses of a human participant. Inclusive (I) indicates the extent to which physical reality is shut out. Extensive (E) indicates the range of sensory modalities accommodated. Surrounding (S) indicates the extent to which this virtual reality is panoramic rather than limited to a narrow field. Vivid (V) indicates the resolution, fidelity and variety of energies simulated within a particular modality (e.g. the visual and colour resolution) (Slater and Wilbur 1997).

Immersion related to presence, in the sense of 'being there', encompasses a reflexive pathway leading to the most suitable paradigm for an analysis of current cyberspace and tomorrow's metaverse, which is phenomenology and postphenomenology. Don Ihde (1990) coined the term 'postphenomenology' as an adaptation of the intellectual practice initiated by Husserl and continued – among other well-known philosophers – by Heidegger, Schütz and Merleau-Ponty. Ihde envisioned the development of information technology and the integrative trend of man-machine relationships but refuted a total merger. Even as an embodiment (I-technology) -> world technology (e.g. a pair of glasses) must be recognizable as such. The hermeneutic relationship 'I -> (technology – world)' and alterity relationship 'I -> technology – (-world)' help explain the different situations and significance of instruments to our species. Considering all these aspects, Ihde states that humans can be immersed in technology as much as physical reality allows: "I am immersed in the surrounding world, but this immersion is as flexible and dynamic as the panorama about me. This is the chiasm, the intertwining of the flesh of which Merleau-Ponty spoke in his last interpretations of perception" (Ihde 1990, 46). Postphenomenology identifies the ways in which technology mediates human-world relations "by co-constituting the subjectivity and objectivity of experience" (Rosenberger and Verbeek 2015, 20). Gardner and Jenkins analyse experiences of digital technologies on a phenomenological basis and find that participants in their experiments react in "varied, embodied ways, translating the data representations into more complex narratives inspired by their embodied experiences" (2015, 24).

The presence in the computer-mediated virtual world has been the object of investigation and analysis for researchers coming from different branches of the humanities for the last three decades. For some, the quantitative measuring and the experimental approach was the most accurate method of investigation. For others, an in-depth analysis with ethnographic fieldwork was the way to acquire critical data. In order to follow the second path, the use of an epistemological strainer was deemed necessary. As a result, phenomenology became one of the most suitable frameworks for the analysis and interpretation of qualitative social investigations offering fruitful concepts such as "intersubjectivity" and "lifeworld" (Schütz and Luckmann 1973), "*Dasein as being-in-the-world*" (Heidegger 1996), or the "bodily experiences" (Merleau-Ponty 1962). Being in cyberspace is ultimately a way of 'being-in-the-world'. Once immersed in a digital existence, the integration in the network represents an opportunity for one's *Dasein* to perceive and share with another – 'experience the other as other'.

Alfred Schütz described the possibility of a life-world as being in a direct relation to intersubjectivity, which comprises our current experiences marked, to some degree, by the experiences of our predecessors (a model perfectly applicable to the virtual world). The social reality which is in our grasp is called the *Umwelt* (environment), where we find our consociates – those who have touched our existence directly at some point. Outside this sphere, there are contemporaries – those who exist in our time but are not (yet) known to us, the predecessor (who passed before our time) and the successors (who will not be born before our passing away). "Someone enters into the sphere of consociates as they approach you and engage in intimate interaction. The world of contemporaries is thus an open horizon of possible consociates" (Schütz 1967, 144). Schütz has the merit of adapting the epistemological approaches of social sciences to the school of thought initiated by Husserl and continued by Heidegger.

Hardesty and Sheredos adopt Schütz's paradigm of social reality with reference to the everyday life-world and apply it to "parallel spheres of social reality that arise in the virtual worlds of multiplayer online games" (2019, 368). According to Hardesty and Sheredos (2019, 369), we can drop the assumption "that everyday spatial proximity is required for face-to-face interactions". Ollinaho's (2018) analysis of "the virtualization of the life-world" focuses on how the paramount reality of everyday life has itself been transformed and now also entails virtual worlds. Our active attention is demanded not only by the paramount reality of everyday life in Schütz's sense but also by virtual worlds. "Through virtualization, another zone of primary relevance other than that of 'here and now' has been erected and has become a part of the life-world of normal persons engaged in the world of daily life" (Ollinaho 2018, 4).

The 'brave new' citizen of cyberspace

The internet offers the possibility of overcoming the obstacle of physical distance when people want to meet and creating new forms of solidarity or advancing common projects. Although these transformations offer new possibilities for constructing public or personal rhetoric and ideology, they can also be targeted by new forms of manipulation. The key players of cyberspace (driven by the pursuit of profit) will always try to shape ideas and opinions of their audience and, ultimately, modulate the decision-making process – a fact that everybody should be aware of – when accessing the virtual world.

In the age of 'feeds' and 'wikis', classic media is no longer the most important provider of information – as it cannot separate itself from an institutional framework, that of an agent which delivers its cultural products to a passive audience. The new online means of information, be they forums, blogs or social media platforms, create the possibility of an ongoing perception reshape or fine-tuning regarding various events. News can be changed directly and spontaneously by those to whom it is addressed. This can happen without the bias of professional analysts or commentators. This new information and these communication technologies hold an intrinsic promise: they have the potential to provide the opportunity for someone to become famous overnight. This is the essence of web 2.0 – the era in which internet is in permanent transformation under the influence of ideas and opinions of contributors – the outcome of this phenomenon being the creation of "virtual communities" (Rheingold 1993). Web 2.0 – a term attributed to Darcy Di Nuci and popularized by Tim O'Riley and Dale Doherty in the early 2000s – encompasses the diversification of communication platforms leading to the ubiquitous social media. Web 2.0 sites "constitute proliferating spaces in which the multiplicity of encounters, intuitions, ideas, uncertain projects, with no tomorrow or with a bright future, esoteric, talkative or influential exchanges, etc., constitute a kind of essential backdrop to give the actors the feeling of being part of the same community, however different they may be" (Aguiton and Cardon 2008, 81).

Sharing ideas and opinions nowadays has become easier than ever with forums or social media platforms such as Facebook, Twitter and Instagram. Keeping in touch and alleviating the longing for someone is made possible through text communication or audio-videoconferencing (e.g. WhatsApp, Skype, Zoom). However, all these networking software products have a dark side. Walking hand in hand with the idea of 'instant popularity', they nourish the vanity of their users fiercely. Moreover, by conceiving a way of monetizing the popularity through publicity, the moral challenges are even bigger. Virtual space seems to be increasingly marked by territoriality instincts and ownership desires.

Territoriality (Klopfer 1969, 81), a central concept for ethology, relates to the dominant-aggressive behaviour of an individual towards the rest of the animals from the same species living in a given space. Human beings have manifested this behaviour since ancient times over private or collective properties. In the information technology era, virtual space offers human individuals a new substrate to manifest their territorial behaviour, but this time, more strongly impregnated with a symbolic dimension, being closely related to the skill of projecting a popular image associated with fame and credibility.

Having a website, a blog or a video channel (individual or hosted by e.g. YouTube or Vimeo) could become, more important for someone's identity and 'social presence' than owning real estate. The popularity gained from this type of virtual territory can be much more fertile than agricultural land or a real estate lot. And the new and rewarding occupation of an 'influencer' is there to prove it. A great help in increasing digital visibility is the '#' sign with keywords attached to a message intended to assign it to a common thread and speed up thematic identification – which can link social media products to audiences previously beyond their reach.

The use of the computer as the primary means of communication has led to the emergence of a phenomenon similar to that of a "public sphere" (Habermas 1962), but in this instance, a digital one. Karin Knorr-Cetina notes in her studies of exchange traders who spend their working day in front of screens that: "Their bodies and the screen world melt together" (2009, 64). Such groups are formed not only around the need to communicate, but also as a 'community of interest' – where members "exchange information to get answers to personal questions or problems, to improve their understanding of a subject, to share common passions or simply to play" (Henri and Pudelko 2003, 485). As Lindemann and Schünemann mention, in this type of community, "although participants rarely meet each other face to face, they nevertheless experience their communication as an encounter with others in a shared space. This space is established by text-based communicative gestures" (2020, 647).

The argument that the internet could create a meaningful civil society depends mainly on its ability to generate 'social capital', which refers to: "components of social organization such as networks, norms and social trust that facilitates mutually beneficial cooperation" (Putnam 1995, 67). To this day, however, the vivid interactions of a virtual community cannot be a substitute for the need for physical contact. Licoppe describes a difficulty to acknowledge "strong ties" formed over the Internet: "The liveliness of these debates is ... a symptom of the difficulty of conceiving of the establishment of strong ties without moments of physical copresence" (2004, 139).

However, there are situations in which such communities develop spontaneously – as a reaction to an event of broad interest. This is the most common way through which, by the power of online communication, virtual communities (Rheingold 1993) arise. Such a collective emotional complex manifested as a spontaneous cyber-solidarity experience ignited by digital exchanges over a significantly dramatic social event can be included in the phenomenological analysis with one condition: having Schütz and Merleau-Ponty as conceptual torchbearers.

The last decade has proven that internet can serve as an arena for the political participation of people who are otherwise not politically engaged. Non-governmental organizations defending the rights of different categories of individuals have found here the best forum in which to express their claims. Even marginalized groups can find new impetus here to become more active. Virtual communities often demonstrate civic engagement through initiatives that address issues of public concern. Xenos and Moy have shown that "human interaction based on web resources has indeed significant political properties" (2007, 708). A particular case of the influence of social media on political positions is its ability to transform itself into an incubator of civic movements. This space provides the perfect setting for spontaneous cyber-solidarities. Several public actions, such as Occupy (Wall Street), Indignados and, more recently, Gilets Jaunes, have been born from the coagulation of ideas and opinions expressed on different social media platforms.

A virtual community is not inherently conceived as a prelude to face-to-face meeting. Hence, with the exception of a real-life community (e.g. professional, neighbourhood, educational), there are seldom direct encounters. Nonetheless, in the case of communities built upon a phenomenon of instant cyber-solidarity around a dramatic event, the physical encounters (in the form of public mani-festations), while random, are unavoidable. However, even in this case, there is a protocol of exchanging opinions and requests among members and those who are trespassing on the 'netiquette' are pointed at and even banned.

The culture of the virtual world has a certain number of repercussions for the social environment: it can provide a particular look at oneself and constitute, at the same time, a source of community cohesion in real life. The different online social behaviours can be attributed to user characteristics, such as the need to belong or for popularity. Since these psychological factors are related to the habits of people who reveal their feelings or thoughts in public and private digital spaces, it seems essential to examine how online users present themselves: including, for example, the amount of detail or the level of intimacy.

In this context, the most anticipated development of the internet appeared – Web 3.0 (the Semantic Web – metaverse) promoted by simulated society platforms such as Horizon Worlds or Second Life – which allows individuals to create and ex-perience their own ideal world with a sensorial immersion amplified by virtual re-ality headset devices. Web 3.0 represents the pinnacle of internet personalization, facilitating so-called total control over every stream a user may receive. Whether this control is genuine and the flow corresponds to an individual's real needs is an im-portant topic of debate for civil society representatives and social scientists.

The growing interactivity of virtual communities opens up promising new av-enues for studying the outcome and propagation of collective emotions (Levy, 1998), the massive use of the internet being the cause and the outcome. Cyberspace repre-sents an excellent opportunity for the most introverted individuals to have a public voice – even by a minimal gesture of affirming 'Like', assigning an emoticon or shar-ing something online. At the same time, these frugal standard expressions bring, for most users, the perverse effect of inducing an emotional superficiality and a sort of cyber-conventionalism.

Scoping the virtual world – methodological challenges

Personal identity can be challenged when accessing the virtual world. In terms of reshuffling the digital persona, anything goes here: an individual can take advantage of this opportunity to reshape one's identity. An internet user can fashion any profile by changing every aspect of their particular features: age, gender, cultural or social background, or even physical appearance (with fake photos or stolen home videos). It is the quintessence of the postmodern view of identity and personality. Players, for example, can look however they like, can have the house and the job of their dreams and even create their own life partner, to some extent, in virtual worlds of games, such as Minecraft or Roblox, or substantially in metaverse manifestations, such as Second Life or Horizon Worlds. Their historical perspective is no less fluid, ranging from an ancient past to a distant future.

Having a universal binary essence (Miller 2018), any digital product online or otherwise makes rapid customization of its form and content possible according to its user's desires. A member, a 'conferencee', uses an online persona inside a virtual community with the purpose of "addressing, befriending, and developing fairly complex relationships with the delegated puppets-agents of other conferencees" (Stone 1991, 105).

The study of the virtual world has – as its main theme – the way in which new technologies influence the culture of certain groups or society in general. This involves the study of the transition to a "post-corporeal world with new social logics and sensory regimes" (Escobar et al. 1994, 216), but also means appraising the fundamentals of the relationship between humans and AI and grasping the social impact of the integration of AI's emerging technologies. Digital anthropology was envisioned in the early 1990s, when Escobar introduced the term 'cyberculture': "As a new field of anthropological practice, the study of cyberculture is particularly concerned with the cultural construction and reconstruction on which new technologies are based and which they in turn help to shape" (Escobar et al. 1994, 211).

Classically designed ethnographies rely on the idea of location. The researcher visits a community from elsewhere and tries to integrate there for a period long enough to observe and describe the different aspects of its daily life. The structural and functional issues of virtual space trigger a questioning of this paradigm. Even before the arrival of Internet, it was the post-WW2 globalization (i.e. the development of communication technologies and the intensification of the circulation of people and goods by ever faster means of transport) that has created the premises for a process of cultural shift with major impact on anthropological research. The cultural reality of a globalized society called for a new approach: a multilocal ethnography – a complex fieldwork built from an objective need to move between different sites. Manuel Castells, in his work Network Society (1996), envisaged the move towards the study of networks with a wide opening of theoretical perspectives. Unlike the classic 'research site', a network is a very dynamic structure, capable of expanding almost without limits. In the same way, it is necessary to prepare for an increased epistemological rhythm: a flurry of short-term fields around the same subject on networks of similar or different communities, rather than engaging in a long stay of exploration, immobilized in the same place à la Malinowski.

One of the first problems that virtual ethnography has to face is the validity of data provided by the subjects approached during online research. First of all, it is necessary to guarantee the confidentiality of these subjects. Of no less importance, is making sure that subjects' identities are real and unique, thus overcoming the problem of multiple identities within a virtual community. In real life (except a twin mismatch or pathological cases) you cannot meet the same person twice in a day and accept you encountered a completely different one just because you are told so. The lack of face-to-face or any visual contact enhances the risks of receiving 'embellished' or false information from our counterparts. The accuracy of information on, for example, age, gender and nationality proves more difficult to verify in this instance than in real life. Creating a digital persona represents the perfect opportunity to reshape an identity by changing all aspects of formal characteristics: age, sex, ethnic origin, occupation, marital status and even physical appearance (by posting retouched or borrowed photos or videos). As Mantovani notes, "[v]irtual reality is a communication environment in which the interlocutor is increasingly convincing in terms of physical appearance, yet increasingly less tangible and plausible in terms of personal identity. This paradox results from juxtaposing a convincing simulation of the physical presence of the other, and the disappearance of the interlocutor's face behind a mask of false identities" (1996, 197). As in the case of real-world ethnographic journeys, the virtual research tends to be more accurate as time goes by and the integration in a particular online community increases. Gaining trust equals a deeper access. Long-stay research and an internally consistent community are nurturing this process in traditional fieldwork. Unfortunately, these conditions are very difficult to meet in the case of virtual ethnography.

A big challenge also lies in the evaluation of emotions experienced in the context of the use of social networking platforms. Future research should consider the longitudinal emotional effects at the individual and collective level and optimize the validity of the results by taking into account the fluid sociotechnical characteristics of the constantly changing virtual world. The AI software has been shown to be able to analyse and even predict, to some degree, the emotional states of individuals and groups. These systems, equipped with extended representations of the structures of social networks, can prove to be useful companions for a researcher looking for scenarios for approaching and analysing the various online communities.

Furthermore, in order to effectively insinuate oneself as a participant observer in cyberspace, to have a 'presence' of some sort of significance for the other members of the community, a researcher needs also to create a persona. This endeavour raises an ethical dilemma – the subject of an ongoing debate in social sciences while studying the virtual world: how far can an anthropologist go by appealing to an embellished profile in order to gain more favourability from various subjects? Does allowing some natives from Papua to believe that the anthropologist they just encountered is related to the white spirit of an ancestor (Leavitt 2000) is more acceptable than participating in Second Life as an active worldwide explorer and show host? Most of all, can there be any correlation made between the answers provided by a subject and the actual personal features they assume? Are these features still relevant for ethnography in such a particular environment?

Each way of conducting online interviews or observations has its own advantages and disadvantages. The study of the virtual is confronted with the disappearance of a major source of data: the vast majority of communications being the textual gathering of information in nonverbal language (facial and postural emotional expressions) is almost impossible. Emoticons and GIFs barely manage to drive the receiver towards real body language impact. Thus, textual online communication can prevent the feeling of 'being there' by lacking instant replies (e.g. brusque interruption by the other, simultaneous overlapping dialogue, choir or echoing remarks) or nonverbal expressions (gesturing, posturing, mimicking). The prevalent textual communication used on social media platforms has a deep impact on ethnographic research (Garcia et al. 2009). Therefore, digital anthropology will gradually enhance the semantic value of its data.

Researchers, as participant observers, are not spared by the emergence of one's emic metamorphosis while accessing the virtual world. This is an essential part of the methodological specificity of digital anthropology. In order to avoid an axiological contamination in a space where one cannot rely 100 per cent on their senses, an anthropologist must promote a virtual imago which should encompass an honest and socially open individual – who does not add their personal bias to the manipulative potential of the cyberspace life-world.

I had the opportunity in my research to study firsthand, through interviews and participant observation, several protest movements in Romania (among which the #REZIST was most persistent) and all their event planning made through Facebook. All observations and interviews I carried on took place both online and in situ (i.e. Victoria Square, Bucharest). The study aimed to provide an original perspective of the involvement of young people in the debates regarding issues of public interest and particularly the participation of students in actions that could be labelled as 'civic commitment'. The main objective was to highlight, through the ethnographic method (observation and interviews), as many aspects as possible regarding the context underlying the initiation and organization of virtual communities that manifested in public space through protest movements and the role that social media platforms had in the formation of spontaneous solidarities and civic awakening. Participatory observation, one of the main methods used by anthropologists, provided important data about the public events in Bucharest during a four-year time frame (2015–2018).

A series of pertinent opinions regarding the impact of 'new technologies' on social commitment were gathered and important reflections on other similar events around the world (such as Occupy and Arab Spring). However, field research that involves participation in protest movements involves certain risks that can prevent, complicate or contaminate data collection. Crowd psychology is inherently affected by a state of suspicion towards possible 'infiltrators' and the label of an agent 'in civilian clothes' is applied almost automatically to people using photo-video equipment (as is the case in visual anthropology) without press credentials. Additionally, personal or equipment integrity can be put at risk in the event of a mêlée with the police. On the other hand, an empathic support for the cause can affect a researcher's objectivity.

Constant participatory observation of the online and in situ activity of the Facebook platforms titled #CorupțiaUcide, #REZIST and #GeeksforDemocracy highlighted several aspects. The intense communication between followers strengthened their commitment, a fact shown through initiatives for different activities, such as photo/video uploads, placard ideas and various announcements. Protesters demonstrating a highly responsible public attitude is manifested: concern for keeping public space clean, preparing and distributing hot tea. The performative hypostasis of the movement was shown through the involvement of some grandiose-dramatic aspects of the protests – the flag of Romania and the European Union (visible from above) formed with mobile phones and coloured paper). An investment in the public perception of the #REZIST movement abroad was also noticeable through the use of banners in English and online messages addressed to European Union institutions and foreign embassies

The diversity of messages and modes of expression in public demonstrations (allegorical floats, street dramatizations, video-mapping) are the product of lucid creativity enhanced by online interactions. This environment serves as an incubator for progressive and even revolutionary mobilizations. This phenomenon was well-understood by the participants in the 2015–2018 protests: they sought to be as present as much as possible on audio-visual or online information channels, generating positive news.

A social movement is nurtured by public support as long as its cause is deemed legitimate, and its representatives stand firmly against any opponent and raise awareness by initiating public events and topics of debate using various communication technologies. Today, this is more possible than ever as email online forums, blogs, dedicated websites and social media platforms are used to strengthen the movement, acquire resources and instigate direct action.

Conclusion – Questions about a possible future for social sciences in the 'brave new world'

Visiting new realms, even for a short period, cannot remain without some sort of a conscious or unconscious mark on someone's world-view. While encountering almost entirely different communities than those to which they belonged, explorers, conquistadores, missionaries or simple tourists found themselves, to some extent, in front of a reassessment of personal values. 'Long-term overseas travellers' – anthropologists – developed a scientific discipline that thrived on discovering cultural differences. However, their intellectual openness did not trigger or facilitate a total shift of their core values.

The new realms based upon digital technologies set new challenges for conducting an ethnographic journey. Senses and logical reasoning can be deceived more easily here. An epistemological adjustment becomes necessary and the phenomenological and even postphenomenological (Ihde 1990) paradigm seems the most appropriate model to be employed in this case – as it allows someone to pierce the very essence of personal traits.

'Being there' in a virtual world, navigating from cyberspace to metaverse, gives an anthropologist the possibility of studying a versatile, almost limitless cultural environment. The scope of such a freedom of action brings out, subject to the researcher's conscience, the necessity of a process of identity reshaping, to be carried out prior to the actual empiric endeavour. The anthropologist becomes a shapeshifter, a metamorph, not in a deceitful way but in a more accommodating one, to the other community members. Consequently, encountering other 'presences', being the participant observer inside a virtual community, represents the most authentic way to appreciate the sizeable impact digital technologies will keep on having on humankind.

Once evolved from the passive internet-user status ascribed in the 'web 1.0' age, the contributive aspect of social media (Loader and Mercea 2011) raised hopes that cyberspace could become that realm free of censorship, opened to public debate, envisioned by the very first students using the internet. Since the 1990s, studies on the significance of the computerization and digitization of information have focused on socio-political aspects (Kling 1996; Katz 1997), communication technologies (Dizard 1997), cultural aspects (Hershman Leeson 1996; Rochlin 1997) and psychological issues (Turkle 1997). The fact that Turkle expresses concern about how we are changed as technology offers us substitutes for connecting with each other face-to-face is of particular interest (2012, 11).

"Digital technologies in continuity and in a more radical way than classical artifacts, modulate the relationship between organism and the environment [...]. This is reflected on us, on the way we perceive ourselves, on our sense of being there" (Cantone 2022, 2). However, the virtual realm for the foreseeable future has a status of non-autonomy in relation to the non-virtual: a casual one (depending on the hardware equipment) and a 'contentual' one – narratives and semantics being "always dependent on the everyday world in which virtual is embedded" (Malpas 2009, 135). Presence can be considered a subjective experience of being bodily or physically located in a mediated environment (Hofer et al. 2015).

As Steuer (1992) argues, presence, more specifically, telepresence, is defined as the awareness of being in an environment, therefore, the subject is forced to perceive two distinct environments simultaneously when perception is mediated by communication technology: the physical environment in which they are present de facto, and the environment as presented through the technological medium.

Having a 'sense of being there' does not necessarily imply a high level of perceived realism and, thus, a high level of physical presence, and even a short journey into cyberspace is sufficient enough to prove it. Immersion is an excellent term and concept to describe the sensation that cyberspace and metaverse users/inhabitants have – that of being present in an alternative environment, in a different realm. As defined in Biocca and Levy (1995), the concept describes a feeling of 'being there': the user is surrounded by an alternative reality demanding their full attention (Murray 1997). Berger argues that "actors synthesize a single hybrid space, in which the virtual space and the space of the body and its physical surroundings are linked to each other" (2020, 616). The design of virtual worlds with ontologies different than the real world are tailored to elicit a particular effect on the immersed user. The power of virtual reality to change ourselves in this manner is usually attributed to the capability of the medium to induce a feeling of presence in the computer-synthesized worlds (Slater and Sanchez-Vives 2014).

"Through culture, humans are always already virtual; ethnography has always been a kind of virtual investigation of the human, and can therefore play an important role in understanding cybersociality" (Boellstorff 2008, 249). The scientific journey into the cultural traits of virtual space is not a new field. It was born almost at the same time as the Internet. But the major shift that can be seen on the ground, with the mass isolation imposed under the threat of the spread of COVID-19, is that the epistemology of virtual space research is becoming a discipline in itself among the social sciences. Its main topics will probably even emerge into new disciplines. It is probable that, in the very near future, the study of, for example, e-democracy, virtual economy and telemedicine, will produce as much bibliographic material each year as their counterparts studying the development of social life in physical space. Just as with the establishment of a lingua franca of the Internet, at least in virtual space, globalization will triumph, and *ethnos* will be replaced by *logos*.

Methodological standards for internet research cannot be static, as technologies and the way they are used are constantly changing. Therefore, new frameworks must emerge as changes to the nature and use of social media make them necessary. The researcher should ensure that an ethical approach is taken to the collection, analysis and reuse of data gathered on social media platforms, as each research context may be unique, with its own ethical challenges.

The aim of such an endeavour would be to create an a priori instrument capable of helping the researcher in social sciences to anticipate and manage any possible diversions that the virtual environment could inflict on the collection and, ultimately, on the validity of data. This instrument should lead to a self-questioning about the congruence of the means and intentions of the researcher while recording and sharing various experiences in the cyberspace of today and in the metaverse of tomorrow. This approach requires, first of all, an appraisal of the extent to which the evolutionary trends of cyberspace and the metaverse, designed by private multinational agents, would be able to preserve the cultural complexity of the human being – apart from the status of a mere user of digital platforms.

A researcher must, firstly, submit to a phenomenological journey to engage better in an ethnographic approach aimed at virtual communities; one must get rid of the customs of the real world and start a reflection on the social impact of the internet in its evolution, on the identity of oneself and others. We do not find ourselves in a world contextualized by the 'social contract', but in the one managed mainly by private actors, whether they are multinational companies or independent collaborative agents. Finally, all these opportunities to integrate into an alternative reality, such as virtual space, should not encourage anomie, a life outside the rules. Ultimately, the consequences could be tragic both on an individual and social level.

Physical and cultural differences always lead to a plethora of attitudinal reactions everywhere in the world. Certain attitudes were deemed unacceptable during the development of human society, and modernity required an almost total acceptance of differences. All the same, this does not represent a sufficient reason to integrate into a world, be it virtual, where any difference which can generate digital presence happens to become a question of contextual choice, without any reference to the cultural origins of an individual. This will only further contribute to cultural homogenization. A researcher looking at the actions of human beings cannot help but reflect on whether it is worth designing a social universe that does not contribute to highlighting and enriching the background of an individual or a group.

Bibliography

Aguiton, Cristophe, and Dominique Cardon. 2008. "Web Participatif et Innovation Collective." Hermès, La Revue, 5 0 (1): 75–82

Biocca, Frank, and Levy Mark. 1995. Communication in the Age of Virtual Reality. Hillsdale: Erlbaum Associates.

Boellstorff, Tom. 2008. Coming of Age in Second Life: An Anthropologist Explores the Virtually Human. Princeton: Princeton University Press.

Bracken, Cheryl Campanella, and Paul Skalski, eds. 2010. Immersed in Media. Telepresence in Everyday Life. New York: Routledge.

Cantone, Damiano. 2022. "The Simulated Body: A Preliminary Investigation into the Relationship Between Neuroscientific Studies, Phenomenology and Virtual Reality." Foundations of Science. https:\\doi.org\\10.1007\\s10699-022-09849-x.

Chalmers, David. 2017. "The Virtual and the Real." Disputatio 9 (46): 309–52. https://doi.org/10.1515/disp-2017-0009.

Dizard, Wilson. 1997. Old Media, New Media: Mass Communications in the Information Age. New York: Longman.

Escobar, Arturo, David Hess, Isabel Licha, Will Sibley, Marilyn Strathern, and Judith
Sutz. 1994. "Welcome to Cyberia. Notes on the Anthropology of Cyberculture."
Current Anthropology 35 (3): 211–31.

Garcia, Angela, Alecea Standlee, Jennifer Bechkoff, and Yan Cui. 2009. "Ethnographic Approaches to the Internet and Computer-mediated Communication."
Journal of Contemporary Ethnography 38 (1): 52–78. https://doi.org/10.1177/089
1241607310839.

Gardner, Paula, and Barbara Jenkins. 2015. "Bodily Intra-actions with Biometric Devices." Body & Society 22 (1): 3–30. https://doi.org/10.1177/1357034X15604030.

Habermas, Jürgen. (1962) 1989. The Structural Transformation of the Public Sphere.
Cambridge: Polity.

Hardesty, Rebecca. A., and Ben Sheredos. 2019. "Being Together, Worlds Apart: A
Virtual-Worldly Phenomenology." Human Studies 42 (3): 343–70. https://doi.or
g/10.1007/s10746-019-09500-y.

Hofer, Matthias, Tilo Hartmann, Allison Eden, Rabindra Ratan, and Lindsay Hahn.
2020. "The Role of Plausibility in the Experience of Spatial Presence in Virtual
Environments." Frontiers in Virtual Reality 1. https://doi.org/10.3389/frvir.2020
.00002.

Heidegger, Martin. (1953) 1996. Being and Time: A Translation of "Sein und Zeit".
Translated by Joan Stambaugh. Albany, New York: State University of New York
Press.

Henri, France, and Beatrice Pudelko. 2003. "Understanding and Analysing Activity
and Learning in Virtual Communities." Journal of Computer Assisted Learning
19 (4): 474–87 http://dx.doi.org/10.1046/j.0266-4909.2003.00051.x.

Hershman Leeson, Lynn. 1996. Clicking in: Hot Links to a Digital Culture. Seattle:
Bay Press.

Ihde, Don. 1990. Technology and the Lifeworld: From Garden to Earth. Blooming-
ton, Indiana: Indiana University Press.

Kling, Rob, ed. 1996. Computerization and Controversy: Value Conflicts and Social
Choices. 2nd ed. New York: Academic Press.

Klopfer, Peter. H. 1969. Habitats and Territories: A Study of the Use of Space by Animals. New York: Basic Books.

Knorr-Cetina, Karin. 2009. "The Synthetic Situation: Interactionism for a Global
World." Symbolic Interaction 32 (1): 61–87. https://doi.org/10.1525/si.2009.32.1
.61.

Leavitt, Stephen. 2000. "The Apotheosis of White Men? A Reexamination of Beliefs
about Europeans as Ancestral Spirits." Oceania 70 (4): 304–23. https://doi.org/1
0.1002/j.1834-4461.2000.tb03069.x.

Lévy, Pierre. 1998. Becoming Virtual: Reality in the Digital Age. New York: Plenum Trade.

Licoppe, Christian. 2004. "'Connected' Presence: The Emergence of a New Repertoire for Managing Social Relationships in a Changing Communication Technoscape." Environment and Planning D: Society and Space 22 (1): 135–56. https://doi.org/10.1068/d323t.

Lindemann, Gesa, and David Schünemann. 2020. "Presence in Digital Spaces. A Phenomenological Concept of Presence in Mediatized Communication." Human Studies 43: 627–51. https://doi.org/10.1007/s10746-020-09567-y.

Loader, Brian D., and Dan Mercea. 2011. "Networking Democracy? Social Media Innovations and Participatory Politics." Information, Communication & Society 14 (6): 757–69. https://doi.org/10.1080/1369118X.2011.592648.

Katz, Jon. 1997. Media Rants: Postpolitics in the Digital Nation. San Francisco: Hardwired.

Lombard, Matthew, and Theresa Ditton. 1997. "At the Heart of It All: The Concept of Presence." Journal of Computer-Mediated Communication 3 (2). https://doi.org/10.1111/j.1083-6101.1997.tb00072.x.

Malpas, Jeff. 2009. "The Non-autonomy of the Virtual." Convergence: The International Journal of Research into New Media Technologies 15 (2): 135–39. https://doi.org/10.1177/1354856508101579.

Mantovani, Giuseppe. 1995. "Virtual Reality as a Communication Environment: Consensual Hallucination, Fiction, and Possible Selves." Human Relations 48 (6): 669–83. https://doi.org/10.1177/001872679504800604.

Merleau-Ponty, Maurice. 1962. Phenomenology of Perception. Translated by Colin Smith. London: Routledge & Kegan Paul.

Miller, Daniel. 2018. "Digital Anthropology." The Cambridge Encyclopedia of Anthropology, edited by F. Stein, S. Lazar, M. Candea, H. Diemberger, J. Robbins, A. Sanchez and R. Stasch. http://doi.org/10.29164/18digital.

Murray, Janet H. 1997. Hamlet on the Holodeck: The Future of Narrative in Cyberspace. Cambridge: MIT Press.

Ollinaho, Ossi I. 2018. "Virtualization of the Life-World." Human Studies 41 (2): 193–209. https://doi.org/10.1007/s10746-017-9455-3.

Putnam, Robert D. 1995. "Bowling Alone: America's Declining Social Capital." Journal of Democracy 6 (1): 5–78.

Rheingold, Howard. 1993. The Virtual Community: Homesteading on the Electronic Frontier. New York: Harper Perennial.

Rochlin, Gene. 1997. Trapped in the Net: The Unanticipated Consequences of Computerization. Princeton, NJ: Princeton University Press.

Rosenberger, Robert, and Peter-Paul Verbeek. 2015. "A Field Guide to Postphenomenology." Postphenomenological Investigations: Essays on Human-Technology Relations, edited by Robert Rosenberger and Peter-Paul Verbeek, 9–41. Lanham, MD: Lexington Books.

Schütz, Alfred. 1967. The Phenomenology of the Social World. Evanston: Northwestern University Press.

———, and Thomas Luckmann. 1973. The Structures of the Life-World. Translated by Richard M. Zaner, and David J. Parent. Evanston: Northwestern University Press.

Slater, Mel, and Maria. V. Sanchez-Vives. 2014. "Transcending the Self in Immersive Virtual Reality." Computer 47 (7): 24–30. http://dx.doi.org/10.1109/MC.2014.198.

———, and Sylvia Wilbur. 1997. "A Framework for Immersive Virtual Environments (FIVE): Speculations on the Role of Presence in Virtual Environments." Presence: Teleoperators and Virtual Environments 6: 603–16. https://doi.org/10.1162/pres.1997.6.6.603.

Steuer, Jonathan. 1992. "Defining Virtual Reality: Dimensions Determining Telepresence." Journal of Communication 42 (4): 73–93.

Turkle, Sherry. 1997. Life on the Screen: Identity in the Age of the Internet. New York: Simon & Schuster.

Westerman, David, and Paul Skalski. 2010. "Computers and Telepresence: A Ghost in the Machine?" In Immersed in Media: Telepresence in Everyday Life, edited by Cheryl Campanella Bracken and Paul D. Skalski, 63–86. New York: Routledge.

Xenos, Michael, and Patricia Moy. 2007. "Direct and Differential Effects of the Internet on Political and Civic Engagement." Journal of Communication 57 (4): 704–18. https://doi.org/10.1111/j.1460-2466.2007.00364.x.

Zhao, Shanyang. 2015. "Constitution of Mutual Knowledge in Telecopresence: Updating Schütz's Phenomenological Theory of the Lifeworld." Journal of Creative Communications 10 (2): 105–27. https://doi.org/10.1177/0973258615597376.

Doing Presence. On the Construction of Relations and Realities in Online Teaching Settings

Marion Näser-Lather

Abstract   *In this paper, I shed light on the digital co-presence in online university teaching during the COVID-19 pandemic and its current discursivisation by students and teachers. Based on an interdisciplinary perspective which combines media theory, sociology, phenomenological and actor-network theory approaches, and drawing on my own observations, surveys at German universities, and statements from academics, I show how digital co-presence is produced by social practices and media dispositives. Furthermore, I point to perceived characteristics and effects of mediated presence, for example, on experiences of community and the self, and argue that perceptions of online teaching are subject to processes of habitualization and appropriation through strategies of making oneself at home. The experience of presence can, therefore, be seen as a culturally changing phenomenon.*

Keywords   *COVID-19 pandemic; online teaching; digital co-presence*

Introduction

Videoconferencing in general, and online teaching in particular, are often considered to be characterized by a lack of 'reality' and, thus, 'presence', as the frequently used term 'virtual teaching' implies. The historian Wolfgang Schmale (2020) points out that online videoconferences do not achieve the effectiveness and productivity of a communicative and reflective situation in the seminar room. He speaks of the importance of "linking communication and sociability through physical presence".[1] Similarly, Gabriela Jaskulla, professor of journalism and media psychology, links the concept of co-presence to physical presence, stating that dialogical learning is a constant exchange, a process. And for this process "the whole person is needed. ... We have to sit together in order to deal with each other. The means of communication of presence make the crucial difference and are also a basis for teaching relationships"

---

1   All German text material has been translated into English by the author.

(Jaskulla 2020). Lecturers and students' opinions differ on how online teaching affects their interaction. Opinions in a faculty survey at the University of Marburg in 2020 ranged from the view that there is little difference between synchronous online teaching and courses in the university classroom to the conviction that teaching is not possible without physical encounters (Philipps-Universität Marburg 2020).

However, when the question of presence is discussed with the help of phenomenological and media-theoretical approaches, it becomes clear that a sense of co-presence within synchronous online teaching is, indeed, created and that the perception of positive, respectively, negative effects of mediation in online teaching situations are subject to socialisation and habitualization processes. Socialization in this context means the existence and the manner of previous experiences with digital means of communication, while habitualization can occur in correspondence with self-images entailing a certain habitus with specific tastes and views, for example, being a tech-savvy gamer.

The cultural anthropologist Stefan Beck (2000) has referred to technogenic forms of closeness and intimacy. Technogenic spaces can, thus, function as dimensions of socialization and create a sense of presence, of 'being there', albeit modified by the mediated environments of digital infrastructures. I will explore this idea in the following, taking the discussions on digital co-presence in the context of university teaching online during the COVID-19 pandemic as a starting point to attempt a conceptualization of digital co-presence with a focus on videoconferences. I try to approach the topic in an interdisciplinary way, taking into account different perspectives, in order to create a basis that can be fruitful for cultural anthropological analyses of digital co-presence in general. Regarding this endeavour, I draw on elements from various theories and studies on mediated presence, taken from information and communication science, psychology, sociology, phenomenology, actor-network theory, affordances theory and the concept of social interaction by sociologist Erving Goffman (2001). Using these approaches, I will show the conditions under which a sense of digital co-presence emerges in online conferences, and the aspects and influential factors that shape it. Based on my own observations as a university lecturer, data from surveys of German students and university teachers (2020–2021) and statements of academics, I will discuss the perceived implications of online co-presence for life-worlds, identities and the (bodily) self. Finally, I propose that presence can be understood not as a state but as an unfolding process of doing presence through social practices in a network of human-technology interactions, and that the experience of presence can be understood as a culturally changing phenomenon subject to processes of habitualization and appropriation. Telepresence, especially the aspects of remote control and the immersion in mediated environments, has already been discussed (e.g. the paper of famous artificial intelligence researcher Marvin Minsky [1980] and the study of communication scientist Jonathan Steuer [1992]). However, there are few studies on the experience of mediated presence in education, (e.g. a paper by education scientist Gail Jones et al. [2015] on presence perception in the case of the usage of virtual reality devices in the classroom), and there is no study on the production of digital co-presence in teaching online during the pandemic. Moreover, focusing on this issue is important, especially in light of the aforementioned heated discussions on synchronous online teaching in which the questions of whether and how far 'presence experience' is possible in videoconferences seem to play centre stage.

Presence has been traditionally understood as temporal and spatial proximity, as physical co-presence. However, (digital) media can provide a liveness and experience of presence that goes beyond physical proximity, for example, through the immediacy of live television (Fewster 2010, 46). This phenomenon, also known as telepresence, has been described as "the extent to which one feels present in the mediated environment" (Steuer 1992, 76; see also Corwin and Erickson-Davis 2020, 170); it is defined not by spatial but by temporal proximity (Fewster 2010, 46). In this article, I want to address different aspects of digitally mediated presence, starting from an understanding of presence as perception and a feeling of 'being there'. As an example, I will take the case of online videoconferencing in the context of synchronous online teaching at German universities during the COVID-19 pandemic and point out its specificities.

Conditions and constraints of digital co-presence

The conditions necessary for a sense of digital co-presence can be described with the help of approaches that decouple social interaction from physical presence. According to theories of presence research, virtual and physical interactions are potentially equivalent and only heuristically distinguishable in terms of subjective perception of presence (Bakardjieva 2003, 293).

The concept of presence can be analysed using the criterion of the subjective sense, which is linked to experiences and feelings in the mediatized environment, i.e. the experience of realism and immersion. From this perspective, presence can be described as an attribution effect, as the construction of the 'reality' of an environment by the people involved in the situation. Communication studies scientist Kwan Lee (2004, 30) defines presence as "a psychological construct dealing with the perceptual process of technology-generated stimuli". As sociologist Shanyang Zhao (2003a, 140f.) points out, "so long as users believe that the assumption is correct, the remote environment remains real to them". Accordingly, following sociologists Cornelia Hahn and Martin Stempfhuber (2015, 16), presence can be understood not as an ontological state but as a process produced by cultural practices.

The online classroom on videoconference platforms, such as Zoom or Big Blue Button, becomes 'real' and 'present' through the content presented on the screen in PowerPoint presentations and videos, and through the interaction of students and teachers – in discussions which are transmitted auditorily and partly visually, in the chat, through excursions to portals like flinga.fi, where mind maps are interactively created by course participants, and, in the case of Big Blue Button, in the shared notes in which single observations or thoughts grow into collaboratively written texts.

Yet, while Lee (2004, 30) has argued that because presence is an attribution effect, "a technology-specific differentiation of presence (telepresence vs. virtual presence) is meaningless, because presence, by definition, is not about the characteristics of technology", there are, as I will show, specificities in the production of online co-presence.

As a starting point, it is necessary to reflect on the nature of the experience of presence. This experience is achieved, to a not inconsiderable extent, by the focus of the attention on a given situation. This attention is given in different ways. Firstly, the subjective perception of presence is linked to sensory experiences and feelings in and with the (mediated) environment. Following phenomenological theories, such as those of Edmund Husserl (1950–52) and Maurice Merleau-Ponty (1974), presence can be linked to perception through the lived body (*Leib*), and bodily experiences through the senses (Fewster 2010, 46). Secondly, experiences of mediated presence also depend on the ability to (inter)act in and with the corresponding mediated environments, i.e. interactivity and the resulting agency or self-efficacy. Thirdly, and related to the other two aspects, we have the impression of presence in synchronous situations of social interaction, as theatre studies scientist Russell Fewster (2010, 46) and cultural anthropologists Anna Corwin and Cordelia Erickson-Davis (2020, 170) point out: in the moment we perceive a situation as social interaction, we are present in it. Erving Goffman (1996, 16) defines social situations as "the scene observed by all those immediately present". When participants are focused on their fellow students' voiced opinions during a course held by online conference, and are compelled to answer, they are certainly 'present' in the situation.

Therefore, mediated experiences of presence are influenced, on the one hand, by the users or participants in the social interaction themselves and, on the other hand, by the media environments and the conditions of interaction they create. These influencing factors configure the way feelings and constructions of meaning are experienced within a mediated environment. They lead to immersion and, thus, to the impression of presence. As film maker Martin Schweser (2000, 23) puts it, media unfold "a reality of their own" that causes "being drawn in", a "dissociation from temporal, spatial and social contexts".

I will now sketch out the conditions mentioned above that enable the experience of digital co-presence: in a first step, I will address the primarily media-related aspects of sensory input and interactivity and their effects: immersion vs. distraction. In a second step, I will discuss the user-related aspect of presence in situations of social interaction. It is important to note that I consider these aspects not as necessary but as sufficient conditions for presence and, simultaneously, as aspects of presence or modes in which presence can manifest itself. However, these aspects are intertwined: the presence of more than one of them, or a greater intensity, should result in a more intense sense of presence.

Digital co-presence as function of sensory input and interaction/control possibilities

To elaborate on the first point, sensual experiences in the mediatized environment, in an adaptation of the concepts proposed by behavioural scientists Bob Witmer and Michael Singer (1998) and Gail Jones and colleagues (2015, 15), I distinguish the components of environmental presence that form sensory-induced immersion, firstly, vividness of surroundings and, secondly, realism, as essential.

The first aspect, vividness of surroundings and people, is related to the perceived sufficiency of information in mediatized contacts, which makes them seem plausible and lifelike (Ermi and Mäyrä 2005). Vividness is achieved by creating a mediatized space based on high information density through sensory impressions. It means the extent to which impressions are enriched within the mediatized space (Steuer 1992, 80). Enrichment has different aspects: sensory enrichment and social enrichment (Lombard and Ditton 1997). It can also be related to sensory breadth as the number of different sensory dimensions, i.e. the multisensory environment and the quantity of sensory impressions, and sensory depth: the resolution of sensory information (Slater and Wilbur 1997; Steuer 1992). Sensory vividness in online videoconferences is created by the contents presented and through the video transmissions of the participants' faces and upper bodies and their voices, while social vividness emerges through the thoughts they share with each other.

Sensual richness might, but does not need to be, related to the second aspect: the realism, for example, of objects and sounds (Lombard and Ditton 1997; Witmer and Singer 1998; Jones et al. 2015, 15). The realism of objects promotes the impression of presence, as 'unrealistically' presented objects impede immersion – they immediately draw attention to the mediated character of the interaction situation due to their appearance, which deviates from everyday experience. Sudden pixelations, image jerks, freezing of pictures or voice distortions can, therefore, abruptly interrupt the feeling of presence in synchronous online teaching situations. The amount of sensory input that engages the senses through visual and auditory data, as well as the representation of motion, may influence the degree to which an environment is perceived as 'realistic' (Jones et al. 2015, 17). The availability of audio and video transmission in online videoconferences could lead to a more intense presence experience. Furthermore, the precise coordination of all these sensory data which allows for a "holistic experience of the virtual environment" is relevant for sensory-induced immersion (Heeter 1992) – which explains why a delay of mimic movement in comparison to the audio data is so irritatingly pointing to the 'virtuality' of the online classroom. In other situations of digital co-presence, such as in three-dimensional (3-D) environments, another factor comes into play: philosophers Paweł Grabarczyk and Marek Pokropski (2016, 32f., 37), referring to computer scientists Mel Slater and Sylvia Wilbur (1997), name the congruence of visual and tactile information and their alignment with the user's movements as a prerequisite for achieving embeddedness in space.

Marwin Minsky (1980) describes the role of (visual and tactile) feedback from sensors which displays the impression of being present and incorporated in telepresence. This is an important part of vividness and sensory impressions, and leads us to the second condition for the experience of co-presence in videoconferencing: interactivity, i.e. the possibility of actively influencing the content and form of the mediatized interaction within the digital environment (Steuer 1992, 80). As Corwin and Erickson-Davis (2020, 166) state, "presence … can be conceived of as the dynamic and ever-emerging interaction of a perceiver-environment system". Gesa Lindemann (2015) identifies the degree of intervention and control over the environment as characteristic of spatial co-presence. Control enables participation (Jones et al. 2015, 15, 17). According to Fewster (2010, 47), this aspect comes to the fore for the sense of presence in the context of social media: here, presence is increasingly defined by participation, rather than by shared physical or even temporal space.

An environment that allows for participation or agency is created in online teaching situations through the interface of input devices, such as a touch screen, microphones, a webcam and keyboard, and output devices, such as a monitor and headphones/speakers, and through features of the videoconference platform which allow for interaction, such as turning one's microphone or camera on or off, the possibility to manipulate the mode in which the faces of the other participants are presented on the screen, and the ability to write something in the chat or the shared notes and draw on the whiteboard. Immersion occurs through the interface-based perceptions of shared reality (Witmer and Singer 1998). An interface becomes a new, partially shared space of digital co-presence that can be appropriated aurally, visually and haptically, and in which one can gain agency, but to whose pitfalls one is also equally exposed, and through which the participants are connected in a network of devices, software and bodies. Vividness, realism and control as preconditions for embodied immersion and, thus, the experience of presence in synchronous online teaching conferences, are fulfilled on a verbal, auditory and/or visual level, and even spatialized in 3-D environments, such as the online socializing platform Laptops in Space (laptopsinspace.de), which was used by some universities during the pandemic for social events.

Immersion vs. distraction

The degree of sensory input, interaction and control can be used to infer the extent of immersion, but also the level of distraction. Distraction, in this context, can be conceptualized as a measure of the extent to which the sense of presence is not given. In addition to a lack of vividness, realism and control, the potential for distraction arises from the interconnectedness of media and user characteristics in multimodal and intermedial contexts. As theatre studies scientists Liesbeth Nibbe-link and Sigrid Merx (2010, 218) point out, "intermediality often addresses various sensory modalities at once, and typically the senses contradict each other". Percep-tual expectations in intermedial environments are sometimes deconstructed and a clash between digital sensory input and embodied presence can manifest, which can lead to experiences of surprise, confusion or even displacement and alien-ation (Nibbelink and Merx 2010, 219). In relation to the online teaching situation, the different private spaces of the participants that one sees during a videocon-ference could hinder immersion. The latter also depends on the functionality of the devices, such as the resolution, sound quality and speed of information flow (internet connection and device performance, i.e. processor speed and random-access memory available), which is one of the reasons for Jaskulla's criticism of online teaching (2020) – she complains about the grotesque distortion of the voice in online conferences.

Of course, external disturbances can also cause distraction, given the fact that immersion is related to focusing on the mediated environment while ignoring the physical environment. Immersion can only occur if part of the physical environment can be ignored by focusing one's attention. As Schweser (2000, 27) said, "it is the selective construction performance of the user that is necessary to achieve media 'vividness'". Immersion can be disturbed by technical deficits or unmediated im-pressions for which there is no habitualization effect – most often by noise from outside, the neighbour renovating their house or children suddenly demanding at-tention in the home-office teaching situation during the pandemic. Such an expe-rience can have the effect that "the space you had imagined has completely disap-peared", as Schweser writes with reference to telephoning. Sensory immersion can be facilitated by technology that helps to block out the physical environment (Slater and Wilbur 1997), such as interface components, for example, noise-cancelling head-phones.

The ability to ignore disturbances is, in turn, influenced by individual factors, such as the ability to concentrate and the "willingness to disregard external stim-uli" (Jones et al. 2015, 17). In addition, acute psychological states of the individual, such as mood, alertness and prior experience, also play a role (Zhao 2003b, 451). It is interesting to notice that, while a manifold of distractions can also occur in class-rooms with physical co-presence, such as noises, high temperature in summer and interruptions, they appear to be mitigated in comparison to the situation of digital co-presence by the fact that the bodily anchoring of 'being here' is more pronounced in the case of physical co-presence because more channels report it to the physiopsychic system.[2]

If the online conferencing situation involves some kind of challenge-based immersion, related to the phenomenon of flow experience, the environment may be more easily tuned out because the trance-like focus on the corresponding task may lead to forgetting the physical space. Media studies researchers Laura Ermi and Frans Mäyrä (2005) point out that such a trance often occurs during gameplay. It should be similar with imaginative immersion – focusing on a narrative like a story (Grabarczyk and Pokropski 2016, 32). In our case: following the content of the university lecture.

Thus, the sense of immersion is influenced, on the one hand, by situational factors related to properties of the mediated environment, such as software, interface and disruptive events, and, on the other hand, by environmental factors, such as temperature, light, sound and smell. However, immersion does not only occur in shared audio-visual online space; it can also reach a high intensity without these modes of perception – related to the third mode that allows the impression of digital co-presence: synchronous situations of social interaction.

Experiences of presence in synchronous situations of social interaction

Cultural anthropologist Marion Hamm (2011, 29) describes how she spent days and nights "as if welded to a screen and keyboard, physically isolated in my shared flat" during her fieldwork on the G8 protests in 2003. She knew her field partners only through text communication and their nicknames, but for her, "an abundance of signs" compensated for the lack of non-verbal signals and acted "as a kind of digital corporeality". As a result, she felt "digitally co-present in the vastness of the hybrid communication space in terms of my experience and actions". Similarly, sociologist Gabriela Eiden (2004, 25) describes immersion experiences when chatting, "that you look at the screen and almost forget everything around you", and linguistics researcher Katrin Lehnen (2020) points out that chat rooms create the impression of spatial proximity. Even in the case of emails, their temporal proximity can create a sense of co-presence.[3]

As we can see from the examples given, the experience of presence can mean parasociality, i.e. being present as a social actor through mediated interaction with

---

2   I thank Zhenwei Wang for the inspiration leading to this thought.
3   I thank Antje van Elsbergen for this observation.

each other, in the case of synchronous situations of social interaction.[4] I, therefore, define social presence, following communication studies scientists Frank Biocca and Chad Harms (2002), as the feeling of being connected to others. Similarly, social work scientist Daniel Houben (2017) links social interaction to philosopher and psychologist George Herbert Mead's idea of mutual interrelatedness (1973). Thus, social presence does not require physical co-presence.

The main conditions for the impression of social presence relevant for online teaching situations are, as can be deduced, firstly, the synchronous sharing of (media) environments (Goffman 2001, 55; Houben 2017), secondly, mutual perception and awareness of each other (Lombard and Ditton 1997; Biocca and Harms 2002; Houben 2017), and thirdly, the ability to react to each other (Houben 2017), as also implied by Goffman's definition of social situations as "that to which a person can turn at a given moment" (2001, 55).

These prerequisites are also found in synchronous online teaching situations: the sharing of environments takes place verbally, auditorily and/or visually through videoconferencing tools, such as Zoom or Big Blue Button, and even spatially through avatars in 3-D environments, such as Laptops in Space. These tools enable mutual perception and awareness, and the ability to react to each other.

Vividness, realism and interaction possibilities – the aforementioned prerequisites for experiencing presence as immersion – also influence feelings of social (co-)presence in mediated environments in the form of visual representation and realistic movements of the other person(s) and their ability to respond to the perceiver in verbal and non-verbal interaction (Heeter 1992; Tu 2002; Oh et al. 2016).

Therefore, the sense of presence in digital communication depends on both the media as dispositifs that determine the conditions of action and the users and their actions, perceptions, feelings and constructions of meaning, which, in turn, are influenced by the media affordances and constraints mentioned previously.

I would like to illustrate what this means in concrete terms in the following section. Drawing on statements about online university teaching during the pandemic, I will reflect on the specificities and effects of mediated co-presence perceived in online conferences that are related to media properties and differences between users in terms of attitudes and experiences.

---

4   These interactions do not have to be confined to human others; co-presence and communitas can also be felt towards non-human actors such as animals or, in the case of games, non-player characters.

Perceived effects of mediated co-presence

Statements from students at the University of Passau show ambivalent perceptions, for example, of concentration. Compared to the lecture hall, 19 per cent of the students were significantly less attentive, 27 per cent somewhat less attentive, and 18 per cent saw no difference. However, 17 per cent also stated that they were slightly more attentive and 18 per cent that they were even significantly more attentive than in the lecture hall (Universität Passau 2020). One reason for the latter could be the reduction in distractions: the 'seminar room' consists only of the interface and the faces of the participants, and conversations between students now take place invisibly in the chat and do not interfere with the main interaction.

However, videoconferencing is often said to be more tiring than physical meetings, a phenomenon that has been called 'Zoom fatigue'. Psychologists suggest several reasons for this. One is that people see themselves constantly and are critical of their own reflections (Bailenson 2021).

Drawing on Jacques Lacan's psychoanalytic theory (1986), one can say that what might happen in this context is that the self-experiences itself in new ways – through the perpetuation of the Lacanian mirror stage. The latter begins when infants recognise themselves in a mirror or other reflective surface. The mirror stage also represents a permanent structure of subjectivity for Lacan. It describes the formation of the self through identification with one's own image. By looking into the mirror, the child develops an awareness of themselves. The mirror stage, according to Lacan, also causes alienation and the splitting of the subject or self into the "I" and the "ego". The "I" is the view of the self in the mirror – the experience of being seen from the outside, by others, leading to the development of the social self. The "ego" is the secondary, narcissistic identification of the self with an ideal that one tries to approach (Lacan 1986, 64; see also Borbach 2022, 8). The mirror stage is updated or perpetuated during online conferences. Normally, one looks in the mirror in such a way that one's own idealized image – the ego – is confirmed; here, one is also confronted with unexpected, permanent (negative) views of the I. People are constantly striving to actively influence the impression they make on others (cf. Ruf 2020). Media studies researcher Christoph Borbach (2022, 8) has called Zoom a "permanent feedback loop" through continuous self-observation. The self-experiences its own presence, as one can imagine, with shocking clarity, the self and the unidealized external image suddenly and permanently converging. As a result, the self can become fragile and is reconceptualized through medialization.

In videoconferencing, the self is, as I would put it, fragmented between the online space where the image of the face is located and where the senses of seeing and hearing are focused – and the body that is there in another, offline space and that sometimes demands attention – when it is hungry or has other needs, such as back pain from sitting too long or freezing. These are private experiences that are not shared with the other people in the digital space, with whom communitas is created only through watching, listening and speaking. Thus, the sensory data and materialities that cause a subject to experience its environment as an empirical life-world have changed.

Related to this, an effect could take place which has been observed in relation to digitization in general. Cultural anthropologist Manfred Faßler (2001) identifies the "complexity of distributed presence" as a consequence of digital networking. Houben (2017) mentions a "dissolution of the unity of body, space, time and self" in connection with the establishment of digital communication. This is reminiscent of philosopher Paul Virilio's concept of Teletopia: "To participate in a teleconference or to be telepresent is to be here and somewhere else at the same time" (1990, 336). Under these conditions, subjects find themselves in a multiplicity of spaces (Borbach 2022, 12).

What is more, visual interaction in online conferencing is said to be an extraordinarily stressful situation because of the intense eye contact: a screen full of faces is looking at the perceiver – this can increase social anxiety because, as communication scientist Jeremy Bailenson (2021) argues, "When a face in the real world comes so close to our own, the brain thinks it's an intense social situation: either conflict or a budding two-way relationship". However, I believe that this dynamic is also likely to work in the opposite way to reduce social anxiety: the faces in videoconferencing are much smaller than in physical presence, so they suggest further distance, and the dimension of physicality, of being bodily in the same room as others, falls away. A side effect of the situation of a screen full of faces looking at the perceiver is that people may even have a stronger sense of the presence of others than in a physical seminar room: the others are not partially covered and at different distances – and so everyone can see and react to everyone else, which promotes feelings of closeness and intimacy.

Bailenson (2021) cites the cognitive load caused by the reduced decodability of communication signals as a third reason for zoom fatigue. Similarly, cognitive psychologist Christian Stöcker (2020) states in a column of the journal *Der Spiegel*: "On moving images the size of a credit card, we humans cannot correctly recognise what is naturally conveyed in a normal conversation: non-verbal signals, facial expressions, small gestures, body posture. This results in a constant, unconscious effort to 'read' the other person".

And this is where Gabriela Jaskulla's (2020) criticism of online teaching comes in. She complains that it is more difficult to perceive and respond to students' needs. It can be argued that a physical presence is most comprehensive in terms of the quantity and quality of sensory information available. More levels of perception are addressed in a given amount of time. Some sensory data are also missing in online interaction, such as olfactory stimuli and body language in its entirety, and, thus, applying the theory of phenomenologist Hermann Schmitz (2007), one can deduce that, to some extent, what can be said to be bodily palpable in terms of atmosphere is missing. On the other hand, there can be an even higher density of information exchanged online: participants use the chat to feed in additional content, such as links, which the whole seminar can see immediately. It is also possible to receive multiple statements in parallel, e.g. answers to questions can be given on two channels at the same time – via microphone and in the chat. In addition, as the names of the participants are visible under the pictures in videoconferences, students can (at least in theory) get to know each other more quickly, which could increase the sense of presence of the other. This could be further enhanced by the insight into the living environment of the participants.

An outlook to the future: habitualization processes

In the discourses on academic online teaching cited above, we find not only very ambivalent experiences and evaluations, but also very strong statements of rejection. Verena Kammandel, a trainee teacher, says in a newspaper article that "Pixel images are cold and rigid and implacable. The digital gaze is lonely" and "the whole seminar doesn't mean anything to me because the image has no atmosphere" (2021). One explanation for this argumentation – which still requires further analysis – might be a centrality of the concept of physical presence to the understanding of academic teaching and the self-image of university lecturers and, on the other hand, to the specific needs of communitisation in the pandemic situation: the longing for physical proximity. As Houben (2017) puts it: "When co-present interactions decrease, and thus interactions become more presuppositional, the importance of bodies and relationships paradoxically increases".

However, it is important to point out the culturality and, thus, the mutability of perception and interaction. The senses are culturally trained in processes of socialization and habitualization (Vannini, Waskul and Gottschalk 2012), as is illustrated by learning about the many flavours of wine, and, therefore, all the experiences, effects and evaluations of synchronous online teaching via videoconferencing that I have cited could change over time. The senses adapt and reconfigure in contact with new mediated environments. While playing a fast 3-D videogame for the first time, one might experience nausea, which, however, probably will not be the case the second time.

The visual sensory impressions relevant to the online conferencing situation are configured differently and given various meanings depending on the experiential background and role requirements. According to social anthropologist Sarah Pink and colleagues (2016), the way in which co-presence becomes meaningful is shaped by cultural contexts and norms that determine how intimacy is expressed and by behavioural expectations.

The corresponding attitudes and, thus, also the perceptions of mediated presence are again individual, dependent on experiences, knowledge and dispositions (see also Jones et al. 2015, 16). Grabarczyk and Pokropski (2016, 25f.) identify the perception of affordances as a key factor for experiences of presence in virtual reality. Affordances – the offers or invitations or the use properties of digital media infrastructures (Norman 2013) – appear in relation to users, their bodies, physical abilities, intentions (Grabarczyk and Pokropski 2016, 34) and socio-cultural backgrounds. This means that a medium offers different things to people with a certain knowledge or interests than it does to others, for example, alongside generational differences and the centrality of digital media for work and leisure.

The experience of media and the benefits that can be derived from it depend on individual preconditions – familiarity with elements of digital interfaces and whether, for example, menus are intuitively operated and user interface offerings are immediately perceived as such. Some researchers have argued that presence is closely associated with the degree to which an individual is willing to suspend disbelief and accept incoming stimuli at face value without close scrutiny (Lee 2004, 47).

The very different attitudes to digital media also play a role. Some social groups that have been familiar with (audio) chatting and videoconferencing for decades have long become accustomed to them. Examples include the military and gaming communities. In our specific case, the readiness, respectively, willingness to accept digital infrastructures as teaching tools – or the lack thereof – is also linked to the understanding of university teaching and what it should entail, as well as to corresponding didactic concepts at universities. There seem to be differences, for example, regarding discipline cultures. In subjects of the humanities, the discussion on bodily co-presence is thought of as being a vital part of not only classroom interaction, but also for the comprehensive education of students as responsible citizens. For other subjects, the transfer of knowledge is paramount, which leads to a pedagogic concept more orientated to frontal teaching, for which a more personal exchange is not as important, as is illustrated by a discussion at the University of Jena between philosophy professor Andrea Esser and professor of business administration Nils Boysen (2020). A conference report from 2020 suggests a change in interaction habits. 'Virtual' meetings were described by some as 'face-to-face' events. The report concludes: "The disembodiment of the concept of presence has begun" (Krischke 2020). Zoom's statistics show a huge increase in the platform's usage. While 19 million Zoom users were registered daily in December 2019, by April 2020 there were over 300 million daily meeting attendees (Iqbal 2020). Borbach (2022, 4), therefore, refers to zooming as a new cultural technique. Citing philosopher Michel Foucault, he states: "The Zoom platform, thus, establishes ... a specific order of discourse, insofar as it technologically predetermines communication, installs viewing regimes and formats visibilities ... Zoom, therefore, evokes a discursive order of prefigured visibilities" (Borbach 2022, 5).

The successive appropriation of technogenic spaces that promote the perception of presence can be understood as the implementation of strategies of making oneself at home, as described, for example, by cultural anthropologist Simone Egger (2014). The following components are relevant for strategies of making oneself at home: a subjectively meaningful (affective) relationship to places, people, things and activities, reliability and security, the possibility of participation, agency and control possibilities to experience the space as something that can be shaped, and the production of meaning through the common, familiar.

Conclusion

Perceptions of presence and interaction are shifting and have been transformed by taking place online. Influential factors that produce different forms of online co-presence are the interplay of media dispositives and users, who create the experience of presence through their actions, perceptions, feelings and constructions of meaning, and their effects on life-worlds, identities and the (bodily) self. As I have shown, different aspects that create and shape the experience of mediated presence are, firstly, immersion through the engagement of different senses through vividness and realism, secondly, interactivity as the possibility of interaction and control, and thirdly, social interaction enabled by the sharing of media environments, mutual perception and the ability to react to each other.

Although the physical immediacy of others is a central component of the sense of social co-presence, I have shown that social presence is, nevertheless, created in distant online settings without physical contact in the sense of touching or being exposed to the physical presence of other bodies – through being 'touched' by their voices, images or texts. Individuals dynamically create presence through their actions, perceptions, feelings and constructions of meaning. As Fewster (2010, 47) puts it in the case of mediated presence, "notions of presence, then, exist increasingly as transitional spaces between the live and the digital more than as an absolute ontological condition".

Mediated presence in online teaching situations entails specific requirements, such as a sufficient infrastructure and the willingness to accept it, and ambivalent (short-term) effects in terms of perceived intimacy, concentration and self-perception. However, the perception of presence is subject to social norms, habitualization processes and strategies of making oneself at home. Presence can, thus, be interpreted not as a state but as an unfolding process of doing presence through social practices and relationships. Its concept will continue to change with the dynamics of use and corresponding framing.

Bibliography

Bailenson, Jeremy. 2021. "Nonverbal Overload: A Theoretical Argument for the Causes of Zoom Fatigue." *Technology, Mind, and Behavior* 2 (1). https://doi.org/1 0.1037/tmb0000030.

Bakardjieva, Maria. 2003. "Virtual Togetherness: An Everyday-life Perspective." *Media, Culture & Society* 25 (3): 291–313.

Beck, Stefan. 2000. "media.practices@culture. Perspektiven einer Kulturanthropologie der Mediennutzung." In *Technogene Nähe. Ethnographische Studien zur Mediennutzung im Alltag*, edited by Stefan Beck, 9–20. Münster: LIT Verlag.

Biocca, Frank, and Chad Harms. 2002. "Defining and Measuring Social Presence: Contribution to the Networked Minds Theory and Measure." In *Presence 2002. Proceed^{in}gs of the 5th International Workshop on Presence*, edited by Feliz R. Gouveia and Frank Biocca, 1–36. Porto: Universidade Fernando Pessoa.

Borbach, Christoph. 2022. "Medienanthropologie: Videochat-Kultur – Corona, Zoom und Paul Virilios ,Terminal- Bürger'." In *Corona und die anderen Wissenschaften. Interdisziplinäre Lehren aus der Pandemie*, edited by Peter Klimczak, Denis Newiak and Christer Petersen, 1–14. Wiesbaden: Springer.

Brombin, Alice. 2022. "Presence in the Interstice. University Students' Strategies to Recreate Social Presence in a Post-pandemic Scenario." (Unpublished Paper presented at the 2022 European Association of Social Anthropologists (EASA) conference, Belfast, 26 July 2022).

Corwin, Anna I., and Cordelia Erickson-Davis. 2020. "Experiencing Presence. An Interactive Model of Perception." *HAU: Journal of Ethnographic Theory* 10 (1): 166–82.

Egger, Simone. 2014. *Heimat. Wie wir unseren Sehnsuchtsort immer wieder neu erfinden.* München: Riemann Verlag.

Eiden, Gabriela. 2004. *Soziologische Relevanz der virtuellen Kommunikation.* Zürich: Swiss Online Publications in the Social Sciences.

Ermi, Laura, and Frans Mäyrä. 2005. "Fundamental Components of the Gameplay Experience: Analysing Immersion." *Proceedings of DiGRA 2005: Worlds in Play: International Perspectives on Digital Games Research*, no. 3. https://summit.sfu.ca/ite m/260.

Esser, Andrea Marlen and Nils Boysen. 2020. "Präsenz vs. Online: Die Zukunft der universitären Lehre." 6 August 2020, in *LAUTGEDACHT. Der Podcast*, produced by Universität Jena, podcast. https://www.youtube.com/watch?v=8EhU1vQeT7Y.

Faßler, Manfred. 2001. *Netzwerke.* München: Fink.

Fewster, Russell. 2010. "Presence." In *Mapping Intermediality in Performance*, edited by Sarah Bay-Cheng, Chiel Kattenbelt, Andy Lavender and Robin Nelson, 46–7. Amsterdam: Amsterdam University Press.

Goffman, Erving. 1996. *Stigma. Über Techniken der Bewältigung beschädigter Identität.* Frankfurt a.M.: Suhrkamp.

———. 2001. "Die Interaktionsordnung." In *Interaktion und Geschlecht*, edited by Erving Goffman, 50–104. Frankfurt am Main: Campus.

Grabarczyk, Paweł, and Marek Pokropski. 2016. "Perception of Affordances and Experience of Presence in Virtual Reality." *Avant* 7 (2): 25–44. https://doi.org/10.26913/70202016.0112.0002.

Hahn, Kornelia, and Martin Stempfhuber. 2015. "Präsenzen 2.0. Zur Einführung in die soziologische Erforschung differenzierter Präsenz." In *Präsenzen 2.0. Körperinszenierung in Medienkulturen*, edited by Kornelia Hahn and Martin Stempfhuber, 7–19. Wiesbaden: Springer.

Hamm, Marion. 2011. "Zur ethnographischen Kopräsenz in digitalen Forschungsfeldern." *Kulturen* 5 (2): 28–33.

Heeter, Carrie. 1992. "Being There: The Subjective Experience of Presence." *Presence: Teleoperators and Virtual Environments* 1 (2): 262–71.

Houben, Daniel. 2017. "Von Ko-Präsenz zu Ko-Referenz – Das Erbe Erving Goffmans im Zeitalter digitalisierter Interaktion." In *Leib und Netz. Sozialität zwischen Verkörperung und Virtualisierung*, edited by Matthias Klemm, and Roland Staples, 3–20. Wiesbaden: Springer VS Verlag.

Husserl, Edmund. 1950–1952. *Ideen zu einer reinen Phänomenologie und phänomenologischen Philosophie*. Den Haag: Martinus Nijhof.

Iqbal, Mansoor. 2020. "Zoom Revenue and Usage Statistics. Business of Apps." Last modified 26 April 2023. https://www.businessofapps.com/data/zoom-statistics/.

Jaskulla, Gabriela. 2020. "Die beleidigende Begrenztheit der digitalen Lehre." *faz online*. Last modified 10 June 2020. https://www.faz.net/aktuell/karriere-hochschule/praesenz-an-hochschulen-die-begrenztheit-der-digitalen-lehre-16809260.html.

Jones, Gail M., Rebecca Hite, Gina Childers, Elysa Corin, Mariana Pereyra, Katherince Chesnutt, and Tim Goodale. 2015. "Teachers' and Students' Perceptions of Presence in Virtual Reality Instruction." In *Recent Researches in Engineering Education. Proceedings of the 11th International Conference on Engineering Education*, edited by Kleanthis Psarris and Claudio Guarnaccia, 15–24. Salerno: University of Salerno.

Kammandel, Verena. 2021. "Warum uns digitale Seminare nicht bilden und enorm Erschöpfen." *faz online*. Last modified 6 March 2021. https://www.faz.net/aktuell/karriere-hochschule/gastbeitrag-warum-uns-digitale-seminare-nicht-bilden-und-enorm-erschoepfen-17225873.html?premium.

Krischke, Wolfgang. 2020. "Wer, wenn ich lehrte, hörte mich?" *faz online*. Last modified 4 September 2020. https://www.faz.net/aktuell/karriere-hochschule/hoersaal-tagung-zur-digitalen-lehre-wird-praesenz-doch-ueberschaetzt-16932042.html.

Lacan, Jacques. 1986. "Das Spiegelstadium als Bildner der Ichfunktion, wie sie uns in der psychoanalytischen Erfahrung erscheint." In *Schriften I.*, edited by Jacques Lacan, 61–70. Weinheim: Quadriga.

Lee, Kwan. 2004. "Presence, Explicated." *Communication Theory* 14 (1): 27–50.

Lehnen, Katrin. 2020. "'Alexa, sing ein Liebeslied für mich' – Nähe und Distanz im Zeichen digitaler Emotionskulturen." Lecture presented at Zentrum für Medien und Interaktivität (ZMI), Justus Liebig Universität Gießen, 3 November 2020. https://www.youtube.com/watch?v=AxTIWumdyhA

Lindemann, Gesa. 2015. "Die Verschränkung von Leib und Nexistenz." In *Die Gesellschaft der Daten*, edited by Florian Süssenguth, 41–66. Bielefeld: transcript.

Lombard, Matthew, and Theresa Ditton. 1997. "At the Heart of It All: The Concept of Presence." *Journal of Computer-Mediated Communication* 3 (2). https://doi.org/10.1111/j.1083-6101.1997.tb00072.x.

Mead, George Herbert. 1973. *Geist, Identität und Gesellschaft. Aus der Sicht des Sozialbehaviorismus.* Frankfurt am Main: Suhrkamp.

Merleau-Ponty, Maurice. 1974. *Phänomenologie der Wahrnehmung.* München: De Gruyter.

Minsky, Marvin. 1980. "Telepresence." *OMNI Magazine* 9 (2): 44–52. https://web.media.mit.edu/~minsky/papers/Telepresence.html

Nibbelink, Liesbeth Groot, and Sigrid Merx. 2010. "Presence and Perception: Analysing Intermediality in Performance." In *Mapping Intermediality In Performance*, edited by Sarah Bay-Cheng, Chiel Kattenbelt, Andy Lavender, and Robin Nelson, 218–29. Amsterdam: Amsterdam University Press.

Norman, Donald. 2013. *The Design of Everyday Things.* Revised and Expanded Edition (2nd ed.). New York: Basic Books.

Oh, Soo Youn, Jeremy Bailenson, Nicole Krämer, and Benjamin Li. 2016. "Let the Avatar Brighten Your Smile: Effects of Enhancing Facial Expressions in Virtual Environments." *PloS One* 11 (9). https://doi.org/10.1371/journal.pone.0161794.

Philipps-Universität Marburg. 2020. "Survey of Staff and Students of the Philipps-University Marburg." (unpublished).

Pink, Sarah, Heather Horst, John Postill, Larissa Hjorth, Tania Lewis and, Jo Tacchi. 2016. *Digital Ethnography. Principles and Practice.* London: Sage.

Ruf, Oliver. 2020. "Zoomen. Zur Konstitution kommunikationsästhetischer Systeme." *Pop-Zeitschrift.* Last modified on 9 November 2020. https://pop-zeitschrift.de/2020/11/09/zoomenautorvon-oliver-ruf-autordatum9-11-2020-datum/.

Schmale, Wolfgang. 2020. "Forum: Digitales Lehren – Interview mit Wolfgang Schmale (Universität Wien)." *H-Soz-Kult.* Last modified March 03, 2020. www.hsozkult.de/debate/id/diskussionen-4950.

Schmitz, Herrmann. 2007. *Der Leib, der Raum und die Gefühle.* Bielefeld: Aisthesis Verlag.

Schweser, Martin J. 2000. "Optionen – Wie sind wir verbunden? Ich nähe einen Knopf ans Hemd." In *Technogene Nähe. Ethnographische Studien zur Mediennutzung im Alltag*, edited by Stefan Beck, 21–37. Münster: LIT.

Slater, Mel, and Sylvia Wilbur. 1997. "A Framework for Immersive Virtual Environments (FIVE): Speculations on the Role of Presence." *Virtual Environments, Presence: Teleoperators and Virtual Environments* 6 (6): 603–16.

Steuer, Jonathan. 1992. "Defining Virtual Reality: Dimensions for Determining Telepresence." *Journal of Communication* 42 (4): 73–93.

Stöcker, Christian. 2020. "Das hilft gegen Shutdown-Erschöpfung." *Spiegel*. Last modified 29 November 2020. https://www.spiegel.de/wissenschaft/mensch/co rona-das-hilft-gegen-lockdown-erschoepfung-a-b4060db6-9c3e-4ecd-97b6-9 0efc9a572de.

Tu, Chih-Hsiung. 2002. "The Impacts of Text-based CMC on Online Social Presence." *Journal of Interactive Online Learning* 1 (2): 1–24.

Universität Passau. 2020. "Digitale Lehre an der Passauer juristischen Fakultät. Ergebnisse der Befragung im Sommersemester 2020." Institut für Rechtsdidaktik. Passau: Universität Passau. www.jura.uni-passau.de/fileadmin/doku mente/fakultaeten/jura/Studiendekan/Digitale_Lehre_-_Ergebnisse_der_Befr agung_im_Sommersemester_2020.pdf.

Vannini, Phillip, Dennis Waskul, and Simon Gottschalk. 2012. *The Senses in Self, Society, and Culture: A Sociology of the Senses*. New York: Routledge.

Virilio, Paul. 1990. "Das dritte Intervall. Ein kritischer Übergang." In *Vom Verschwinden der Ferne. Telekommunikation und Kunst*, edited by Edith Decker and Peter Weibel, 335–46. Köln: DuMont.

Witmer, Bob G., and Michael J. Singer. 1998. "Measuring Presence in Virtual Environments: A Presence Questionnaire." *Presence: Teleoperators & Virtual Environments* 7 (3): 225–40.

Zhao, Shanyang. 2003a. "'Being There' and the Role of Presence Technology." In *Being There: Concepts, Effects and Measurement of User Presence in Synthetic Environments*, edited by Giuseppe Riva, Fabrizio Davide, and Wijnand Ijsselsteijn, 137–46. Amsterdam: Ios Press.

———. 2003b. "Toward a Taxonomy of Copresence." *Presence* 12 (5): 445–55.

Riding Tools and Spiritual Excursion: Modes of Human Presence and Tool Usage

Jung Yeon Kim

Abstract *Tools, can they build space for human consciousness to dwell? This article discusses a semantic expansion of immaterial worlds, through tools functioning as symbolic indicator of 'another world.' Comparing ritual objects as ancient mediator models of an immaterial world, and Virtual Reality (VR) tools as a new alternative reality generator, we will argue how they help transport our mind and body to unknown spheres, generating different frameworks of belief, and ultimately fashion accommodation for multifaceted posthuman presence on our conceptual world map.*

Keywords *Perception of reality; tool; modelling of immaterial world; production of belief; human presence*

Introduction

Late afternoon, July 2017, a shaman stepped down from blades known as *Jack-dou* after his last performance in a daylong ritual. As if returning to Earth, two persons held his arms in help. In a small room, he washed his face with a towel, flopped on the floor, and showed us his bare feet, unwounded. In Korean shamanist tradition, it holds proof of the *General* spirit's miraculous efficacy. To me, this performance recalled the scene of a male gamer running on a Virtual Reality treadmill, gripping "pistols" with two hands. He was shooting monsters in virtual space, to cast them out. For a shaman, *being possessed* is a term commonly used by third parties, as might *being immersed* for the gamer. Apparently and chronologically so disparate, what common points can we gather?

Being, from here to there

As the anecdote hints, this article aims to discuss the mode of *presence*—a provocative subject since the pandemic—as Latour suggested, one year before his passing, that we think about our planetary experience of the "world after," yet to be (Latour, 2021). Taken as a philosophical issue, we want to unfold its essential prerequisites, unpack various modes of presence as mediated by humans' use of tools. In what follows, I will discuss how this process changes and *frames* our notions of what is real and constitutes the real world. However sibylline, "being here" posits those first two preconditions of presence: a being and its environment. If, in anthropological focus on the interaction between mind and body, which generates our sense of self, the "being" is inevitably human, by the second term "here" we refer to its surroundings: the "*lived world*" where a "*lived body*" considers itself to be psychologically located.[1]

As perceived reality "*here*" can be no mere space-time variation of physical surroundings. It also implies subjective interpretation of given context, as a background where continuous internalization and exteriorization of mental and physical activities would occur and intertwine with each other. Merleau-Ponty regards *space* as a means by which the positioning of things becomes possible, and lays stress on its "*universal power*" enabling all things "*to be connected* (Merleau-Ponty 1945, 281)." In other words, the context "*here*" is continuously being woven through mutual interchange of all inputs and outputs between *self* and *world*, in which a never-ending narrative of human *presence* is established. It may be understood as an *Umwelt* construction within the *Lebenswelt*, that is to say, of a self-centered world in intersubjective life-worlds (Husserl 1989, 93).

This process of engagement of the human with his environment is surprising. Beyond the passive form of self-presence in a perceived environment, mankind has been involved with its surroundings in more direct and active ways. Tim Ingold sees building activity as "*part and parcel of life in an environment that is already given in nature, and that has not itself been artificially engineered*" (Ingold 2000, 180). His observation on the "*construction of environments and making worlds*" gives an idea of how this context is naturally made and modified in physical existence. Comparing mankind's with beavers' ways of building dwelling space, he characterizes intentional design, particularity of human constructions, as enacted by a "*self-conscious decision process*" (Ibid. 173–75). This would acquire more evidence when we consider the amplitude of human toolmaking—made, or *co-opted* according to Ingold, prior to the material realization, as we find a functional quality in its use. Tools serve a purpose and become a created part of the physical environment.

Going further, no doubt with desire for immaterial emancipation from our physical body or bodily experience, man has endeavoured to extend the contextual background of his world. In backing away from physical reality as the basic notion of perceptible environment, we easily run across cosmological ideas of a spiritual world,

---

1   The lived body, as described by Merleau-Ponty, is distinguished by an objective and physiological presence, and would refer to "the body experienced in a non-objective way" such as connects the self to the world.

oldest archetype amongst immaterial worlds, occasionally labelled as illogical, heteroclite or unjustified (Servier 1994, 22). Whether ritual techniques or their material supports, to the very tools chosen for functional quality and solid construction as intermediaries with the spiritual world, are assigned metaphoric significations covering over or containing their 'irrational' structure.

If such archetypes of an immaterial world persist in human imagination and belief and broaden conceptual life-fields,[2] these denominators may be applied in search of a contemporary immaterial version by which to extend our physical world. That explains the parallel position of a virtual sphere, digitally cybernated, as legitimate counterpart to religious notions of spiritual reality [Image 1]. Especially when its tool is *Virtual Reality* gadgetry, which creates photorealistic surroundings only through digital language, this comparability regards a genuine and more concrete way of constructing intangible environments.

Image 1: Three semiotic spaces, as context of our experience, connected by use of tools. (Diagram by author.)

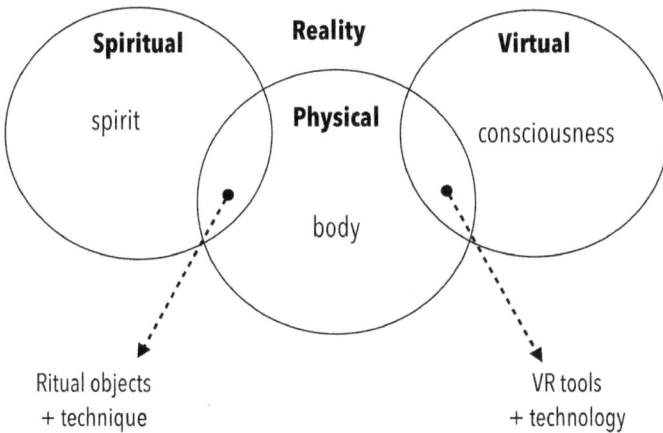

Even though potentially dismissed as mere artificial illusion created by digital equipment or irrational credence vis-à-vis the mythical phenomenon, these tools assume an equivalent role as "mediator" for each conceptual sphere, that help provide access to each immaterial universe. From them can be deduced a map of *semiospheres* comprising three conceptual spaces as inhabitancies of neo-humanity.[3] The latter

---

2   As for Taussig, "this strange world of reality-copy" (Taussig 1993, 103) "extends out"—to borrow Chapin's words—"in all directions."

3   The Semiosphere is certainly not a physical or imaginary space, but a "world of signs and constant communication processes" which affords a "condition for the construction of a world-image or of a world-narrative" (Pier 2018, 267–74). Also, it opens up "the possibility of a spa-

is mediated by "animated inert objects"—ritual and technological—which create a new model of *biosphere* allowing the *noosphere* of human consciousness to install, even attempt union with and be constantly renewed, in relation with such tools.[4] This comparison may let us discover diverse modes of presence of human "being," moving back and forth between two worlds, both intermediated by tools. Named spiritual reality and virtual reality, those immaterial spaces are to be understood as extending the physical dwelling.

Then how do we get there?

The physically enlarged lived world spheres follow no exceptional pattern to be found in traditional conceptions of spiritual world or virtual reality. For example, retracing ancient Pavlov cartography engraved on a mammoth's tusk (25000 B.C.) through the very first mappa mundi atlas of the oceans, then aerial maps and astronomical geographies, one can easily understand the progressive extension of our image of the world, where the physical presence of humans has remained consciously located (Rooney 2018, 11).

Regarding such fearless attempts to discover unknown environments, those expansions in multiple directions were inevitably accompanied by surpassing inventions in means of transportation and relevant equipment. For example, locomotive tools such as ships, air- and space-craft all contributed to iron out atmospheric discrepancies, and effect a change in orbit regarding the use of time and space. If, for Denègre, cartographies define the "accessible world," they also imply a saturation of discovery and pose spatial limits (Denègre 2005, 36–7). Through the custom of repetitive constructions and deconstructions of architectural habitats, so-called modern man has early understood from toying with its plastic globe, the impossibility of further relocation of the body from the soil.

In the same vein, a new generation of mappa mundi [Image1] provides a habitat where the immaterial presence of our modern selves may be settled by tool usage, that Leroi-Gourhan interpreted as "domestication of space and time" (Leroi-

---

tial modelling of concepts that don't of themselves possess a spatial nature" (Lotman 1973, 310). If narrativity is an important cornerstone that underpins the semiotic structure of each culture's 'spiritual world,' it is also clear that virtual environments built by digital language constitute representative space made purely of "signs and communication." The term "semiosphere" juxtaposes itself with other conceptual spheres such as "biosphere," "geosphere" or "noosphere." Nevertheless, I borrow this term as "sphere of commonality," pertaining to three worlds: spiritual, physical and virtual, which can be verbally conceptualized but remain heterogenous in terms of material aspect.

4   The biosphere indicates the sphere of living life and the term noosphere, developed by Vladimir Vernadsky and Pierre Teilhard de Chardin, refers to the 'world of human consciousness and reasoning.'

Gourhan 1965, 135). A corresponding series of implements appropriate for each world sphere, indicates in chronological order each symbolic human characteristic, such as consciousness of spirituality, physicality, and projected rationality.[5] As in the first row here [Image 2], a group of head coverings, objects symbolically linked to each other under "headgear," represent such triple perspectives focused on the human spirit, the physiological brain, and cognitive processes of a VR user.

From among them two objects, the ritual mask of Dan tribe and VR goggles were selected for comparative study, as contrasting tools, which nevertheless both engage human consciousness for "immaterial expansion." Ostensibly two of the headgear are useful as "tools," assuming polyvalent social functions such as entertainment, religious ritual and community welfare. For example, in the Dan tribe culture of Ivory Coast, one can consult *Ge*, a term which signifies both their ancestor spirit and the mask itself. Individual masks of multifarious persona can be endowed by their intermediary genu spirit, not only for religious rites, through different types of *Ge* mask: a highly sacred *Gegbadë* deals with sorcery and healing, while *tano ge* (singing ge), *tankë ge* (dance ge), and *trukë ge* (comedian ge) provide entertainment, and the mask of wisdom, *gegn* is known to tutor and direct young people in their behavior (Reed 2003, 76–82). On the other hand, a wide range of modern VR technology applications can be found in practically equivalent domains: medical treatment, entertainment, religious worship, and education, by revamping the way we engage with related activities. Beyond VR's initial usage for indoor entertainment, psychologists, neurologists, and surgeons apply its tools for therapy and operational training, and some churches have even initiated VR worship.[6]

---

5   Henri Corneille Agrippa's idea of "triple worlds" also classified the world according to planes: celestial, material, and intellectual (Servier 1994, 21).

6   The Life.Church in America is a multi-location TV-based mega-congregation which initiated a VR service, offering online worship through the World Wide Web since 2016.

Image 2: In a conceptual division of body and mind, those objects placed in chronological order represent each contextual sphere of human presence, such as in spiritual, physical, and virtual environments. (Diagram by author.)[7]

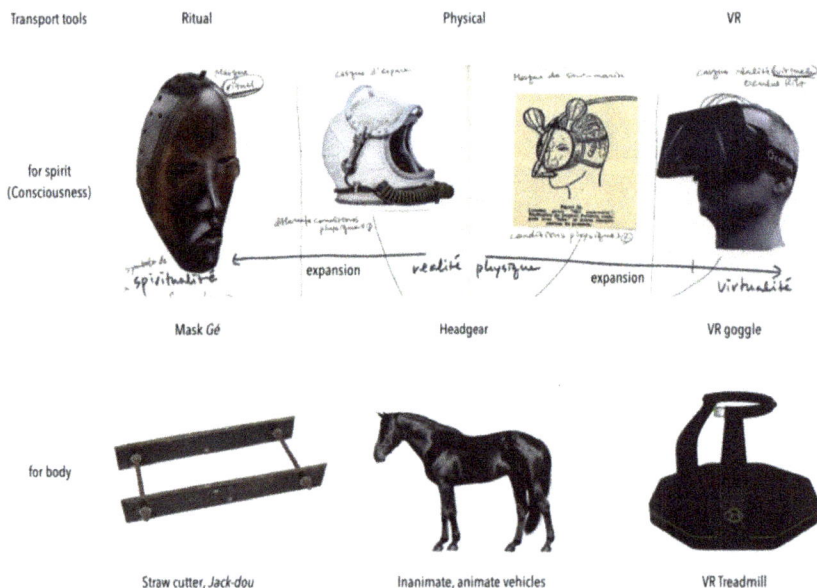

Attention however should be given to *"what individuals experience through those tools,"* often overshadowed by their functional use: as *medium* for the afore-mentioned *Ge*, *media* for the latter. In focusing their mental shift towards extended reality, the ritual mask and VR headgear should be considered as representatives of multi-semantic objects, engaging particular cognitive states of *beingness* beyond their social functions, to be distinguished from headgear used only for physical protection in specific environments [Image 2].

Firstly, whether regarded as vehicle of spirit possession, or as a mimetic « faithful copy » reproduction of a spirit image (Taussig 1993, 52; Merril 2004, 23), the ritual mask is not only a figurative representation of a spiritual existence, but also an embodiment for the wearer who *"becomes"* and *"is"* what is represented (Pernet 1992, 116). As a *Ge* bearer describes, in an interview that I had conducted: *"The mask receives information and transfers it to people, it comes in the form of winds, in the form of reverie...,"* in the Dan tribe's culture, sacred mask bearers are supposed to embody ancestors and sometimes even fall into a trancelike state, even of wild and occult atmosphere, to the sound of shamanic taboret drumming.

---

7   Image from 'reality and tools' project [https://jyeon.com/2017/02/02/realite/].

If a mask effuses a stereotypic sense of *persona*—the shielded veritable character and face of a person—(Mauss 1938, 277) this appears also through visual representation and the continuous phenomenon of *human becoming* (Ingold 2014, 20; Haraway 2008, 244) in virtuality, equally intersected on a VR headset. An individual user, replicating *autogenesis*, may experience union with his avatar, as a digital version of the self that exists 'within' the interface (White 2006, 120), through 360° optical immersion in graphically realistic *trompe-œil* imagery, enhanced by multi sensorial effects. This alliance, based on the stereoscope principle, establishes the physiological mechanism of binocular relief perception which creates the sensation of being in a three-dimensional virtual space (Cahen 1989, 8).

Nevertheless, ponderous bodies, in pursuit of such dematerialized worlds, oblige us to seriously reflect on human ontology. If those headgear were to liberate the human spirit from the materiality of the body, the next group might activate translocation, or transcendency of bodily presence from its materiality [Image 2, p. 62]. The pursuit of locomotion in physical reality, using living tools such as in horse culture, can be considered the very first geographic transfer of the human body, that facilitated early extension of territory, and rapid advances in successful adaptation to any inhospitable environment (Kelekna 2009, 2–3). For equivalent functions, a ritual *Jack-dou* object and a VR treadmill both meet a semantic purpose in extending physical environments that illustrate the following question: "*how escape laws of gravity and materiality?*"

Jack-dou on the left [Image 2], for example, which had been traditionally used as an agricultural implement in Korea, also serves as a ritual object in shamanic performances. It is composed of two sharpened blades, on which the shaman walks and dances without injury to his feet, due to protection afforded by the incarnated spirit. The more we see phenomena that defy laws of physics, the more the shaman's credibility and spiritual power is justified. Shamanic experiences overlap presences of spirit and self. The shaman's physical presence, feet weighing down on two blades, pertains not to physical properties of their sharpness, but to a liminal state where his bodily presence can be governed by the incarnated spirit's will. The ritual itself demonstrates the powerlessness of flesh and blood, and the limits of physical being.

Virtual reality has been criticized for its nuance of Cartesian duality, somehow reinforced by replacing the experiential body by a virtual body supposedly governed by the mind (Murray and Sixsmith 1999, 318). Although precursors such as *Sensorama* targeted total immersion,[8] VR technology has focused mainly, to control the mind, on the faculty of vision. However, since reliance on visual information has proven incomplete, VR technology adds hearing and touch (*Ibid.*, 317). Going further, flexible

---

8   Invented by Marton Heilig in 1952, Sensorama is considered the first "cinema cabin" closest to current VR principles to attempt the creation of a new environment by amalgamating multiple sensorial stimulators.

sensors and exoskeletal devices are now used to develop fuller potential, to reproduce the whole body or its parts in virtuality. Haptic gloves, but also a VR surfboard
or omni-directional treadmill [Image 2], are representative VR accessories for synchronization of a player's and an avatar's body represented on Immersive screens.
Also, this cultivation of a "virtual ground" through VR treadmill or vibrating floor is
an innovative change that confers spatial-dynamic quality such as we experience in
physical environments.

Spatial quality of environment

These brief observations bring us back to the physical object itself: tools, although
tangible as wooden, steel, or plastic artefacts, manifestly encourage us to imagine
hypothetical spaces through multi-sensorial experiences. First, how might these intangible worlds acquire spatial quality as environment? By analogy to human construction, we apply what Ingold calls *building perspective* and *dwelling perspective* (Ingold 2000, 185), whose congruity can be found equivalent on closer inspection to notions such as "built environment" and "embodiment as mode of dwelling." While the
former requires, as in shamanism and VR technology, the spatial permanency of habitual surroundings, the latter would imply temporality and a migratory propensity
as possibilities of being else (Malik 2019, 561–63). How then would these immaterial
worlds perdure as a built environment shared by multiple *dwellers*?

Building

> "In my Father's house are many
> mansions" John 14:2

In his opus "*Milieu and technique*" (1945), Leroi-Gourhan fundamentally distinguishes
between two milieux—external and internal—in which technique would be "*implicitly retained.*" While the value of the first, external, can be understood as "*everything
that materially surrounds man: geological, climatic, animal and vegetable environments,*" the
second, internal, manifests itself at the moment of technical execution and is confined to "*what constitutes the intellectual capital… an extremely complex pool of mental traditions.*" (Leroi-Gourhan 1945, 333–34.)

However, the famous allegory of a cave represented in Plato's *Republic* implies
that our perceptive interaction between external and internal milieux can be controlled by a framework placed between them. It tells a story of prisoners, living in
caves, who cannot see anything happening behind them, merely the shadows cast
on the cave wall in front of them. Shadows become the prisoners' sole "reality," so
long as they stay inside. The dialogue, between Socrates and his interlocutors, im-

plies the vanity of a world view relying on man's sole perception through his senses (Plato 1933, 144–49).

This epistemological reflection evokes what users detect in VR goggles whose universe also resembles a miniature cave, where our eyes are enchanted by the reflection of images imitating a physical world. In this phantasmal space, the two environments are practically super-imposed: the internal milieu is shaken through our vision and consciousness, inasmuch as it is encased by the digitalized external milieu. In other words, photorealistic images in graphic pixels offer a space mechanically integral to the object, but semantically placed as external milieu, nevertheless extraneous to actual physical surroundings. The internal consciousness of man, psychologically charged in the virtual performing of the task, is therefore experiencing layered realities, firstly in the virtual space and secondly in the external physical surroundings.

Both VR and even shamanic embodiment denote this bifold structure of "environment within environment" as a metaphoric cave. In other words, it consists of an enclosed inner space wrapped by outer space, constructed like other human architecture. As Ingold writes, "*the forms that people build arise within the current of their activity... as a practical engagement with their surroundings*," this division gives VR a theoretical quality, as radical phenotype of human constructions, built for psychic activities (Ingold 2000, 186).

How about inside? The panoptic view of interior structures could be explained by the famous phrase of Clifford Geertz: "*Man is an animal suspended in webs of significance he himself has spun.*" In both Ge and VR, the first step starts by preparing a scenographic field with metaphoric objects, to make a creative ritual framework (Goffman 1974, 21), suspended as liminal phase between physical and immaterial realities (Turner 1987, 107).

Symbolic scenography and technical mediation as requisites of visual interaction follow a pattern of theatrical performance, also defined in social ritual (Brandstetter 1988, 38). As in theatrical scenography, objects are distinguished according to their level of metaphoric sense: displayed and nominated, fantasized, subject to semiosis, etc (Pavis 2008, 172),[9] to create narratives and invoke the *yinan* spirit. Likewise, the Ge apparition requires semiotic props, such as throwing kola nuts, a square tin plate, or a short sword half stuck into the ground. A dramatic space starts to unfold by ritual authorization and such manipulation of meaningful objects, while the

---

9   Pavis classifies objects in theatre from "displayed objects (focused in materiality)" to "evoked objects (focused in spirituality)" as following: natural elements, non-figurative forms, legible material, concrete objects, displayed and nominated objects, those only nominated in-text, fantasized, sublimated or subject to semiosis. In ritual, objects display more of the last 4 to 5 characteristics, inclining them to be understood as "evoked objects."

Ge wearer waits for an appropriate moment to leave the sacred house after music is played to solicit spirits.

Similarly, developments in *Jack-dou* ritual also display identical features. Prior to the main *Jack-dou* rite (*Jack-dou-gut*), a ritual enactment of hunting through story-telling (사냥굿, *Sa-nyang-gut*) originating from *Hwang-hae-do* region, is performed. To begin with, a plate filled with dishes or animal sacrifice to feed carnivore spirits is placed in a retired dark spot of the room, since according to scenario hunting has not yet begun. From this collective web of symbolic props emerge the boundaries of dramatic liminal space, as mentioned, symbolized, and articulated by predicative narratives (*Ibid.*, 142). In such a context spectators follow the performance passively throughout.

In a technical perspective, many VR games are supported by the algorithms of Artificial Intelligence (AI). Mainly based on autonomous methodologies such as Machine Learning (ML) or Deep Learning (DL), they create user experiences from path finding to variable context generation.[10] On closer examination, VR reproduces reality as a rendering of familiar objects from real life through graphic components and 3D modelling. The setting-specific meaning demands symbolic decoding: such as, in its commonsensical use, a ball to be thrown or a button to be pushed. With synchronous sensory feedbacks, based on eye- and head-motion tracking sensors, users can actively engage in each scenario. Hence, to follow the algorithms' open narratives, spectatorship is considered as bilateral and critical, compared to ritual performance or theatrical spectacles, since VR users are simultaneously performer and spectator in interactive mode, communicating mainly by visual recognition (White 2006, 115). For this reason, representational design and interactional design—actions and subsequent reactions required for players with represented information—are considered key points, as with other non-immersive interactive contents (Sedig 2004, 1030–32).

Could then VR technology also cater for multiple performer-spectators? Public ritual is known to enhance commitment and shared belief between participants (Etzioni 2000, 45), as the co-presence creates a perception of consensus, a sense of social validation and confirmation (Knottnerus 2010, 41–2). If the early use of Internet technology as "collective ritual" has been considered to inevitably influence levels of focus in attention, pace and interdependency (Ibid. 50–5), AI based on VR technology has been oriented to understand complex systems of collective human intelligence, using virtual or robotic simulators (Cipresso and Riva 2015, 177).

---

10   Anonymous author, "AI in Virtual Reality," The New Frontier of Intelligent Reality(IR), IEEE International Conference of Intelligent Reality (2022), [https://digitalreality.ieee.org/public ations/ai-in-virtual-reality].

Image 3: Recent versions of fully immersive VR contents are offering collective activities in shared virtual space. (Photos © by courtesy of BackLight – Studio VR)

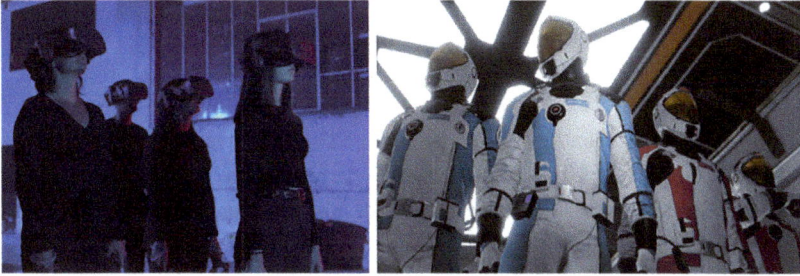

The VR goggle interface, generally dedicated to one individual, is markedly limited in perspective and restricted in quality with regards co-spatial environments.[11] However, recent VR content also offers collective experiences in virtual space, comparable with spectators of ritual who affirm their conviction vis-à-vis mystic phenomena, not only with virtual AI avatars, but also with other co-present human witnesses. *Eclipse* [2017] for example, created by French VR contents developer Back Light Studio – VR, is a hyper reality game in 4D,[12] characterized by collective full body immersion [Image 3].[13]

Four players embody spaceship crews and collaborate talking and moving around between cockpit, hangar, and spacewalk in an area of 15m² (323ft²) which can appear 10 times bigger in virtuality. That demonstrates that virtual space can offer similar levels of interdependency, bonds of sympathy, quasi-physical and emotional co-presence as can be experienced between physically co-present collective users, through verbal communication in the flesh.

---

11   Interview with Frédéric Lecompte, founder of Back Light – Studio VR, 8th Nov. 2022.

12   4-dimensional Virtual Reality digitally incorporates the user's physical body within a virtual environment. If images in VR goggles create a 3-dimensional optical illusion, 4D adds physical synchronization with devices such as VR treadmill, VR motorcycle, or vibrating floor which help users to experience the physical sensation of body movement with haptic feedback.

13   http://eclipsegamevr.com/en_us /eclipse/

Dwelling

I.

"Remain in me, as I also remain in you."
John 15:4

If the VR device's dependency on *"external sources of power"* places it in the machine category which *"do require human direction"* to perform (Mitcham 1994, 162), the reliance of ritual objects on the external energy of spirits to operate through a shaman's bodily techniques certainly establishes a comparably interesting analogy.

The meaning of *dwelling* therefore embraces a broader Broder sense through a performer's spiritual or cognitive embodiment, and a sense of presence or co-presence. In this former, a shaman's body can be seen as an environment "built" for the spirit's "dwelling," which implies putting his own personality in abeyance.[14] Meanwhile, the *Ge* mask wearer tells of his experience as of a sensorial architecture: *"Once you are designated, the force which is given, there is a feeling which is particular, not like the others, the wind which you receive and the information which you receive, there is a technique which is developed in you to receive it."*

To receive such *dwellers*, a Korean shaman begins a summoning process for the *Jack-dou* ritual. Ahead of the ritual his drummer explains: *"When he shows us the performance, it is not he who does it, when he dresses in this costume here, and through that the god-spirit will make a gang-sin* [강신:降神, overshadowing], *it will enter his body...."* He changes into another costume, in order to summon a specific ancestor spirit. The *Gu-gun-bok*, a costume the interviewee shaman wore, had made of him a *Satto* official.[15]

One of the well-known stages to be performed beforehand, is called *coaxing the Jack-dou*. Dangerous moments occur when the shaman strikes his arm or leg with sharpened blades, announcing the arrival of a spirit, its protection over his body and implying the divinity of *Jack-dou*. At the moment of the possession, it becomes more intense, as described by Daniel Kister: *"An initiatory shaman, dressed as the Spirit General and in some degree of trance, "rides the blades"..."* (Kister 1997, 17). The Korean shaman interviewed by your author also recalled his very first experience of losing bodily control: *"I still had all my head, but I started bouncing frantically for no reason. I thought, jumping up, 'Say, what's happening to me? This is no joke'."*

In relation to VR, the state of being possessed can be a symmetrical designation of technological embodiment, where users feel body ownership, a sense of agency in

---

14   Or, as Malik pleads, accepting the "possibility of a multi-dimensional, porous, permeable, fluid identity, self, even 'no-self' or self as 'no-thing'." (Malik 2020, 566.)

15   The 'Satto' is a transformation of "Sa-do [사도 ; 使道]." It generally designates the former title of the Governor of the commune who was responsible for collecting taxes.

the synchronous avatar (Ehrsson 2012, 783). The corporeal representation on screen becomes an element of construction in a virtual arena. Embodiment of an avatar can therefore signify *"framing the body"* (Murray and Sixsmith 1999, 322), as bounded by the limits of virtual activities. It is the injection of human intelligence to an avatar's body, and of artificial intelligence to ours, that combine to create a humanoid of digital spirit.

The level of integration to a virtual body has been through different phases of development from non-immersive, semi-immersive, to fully immersive (or full-dive), until VR achieved highly realistic simulation for users, mobilizing all their movement-enabled sensors. This latest version allows total immersion with detection of users' corporeal movement and their avatar replacement. If a shaman simply chooses a costume to summon a specific spirit, a VR jumpsuit such as *Teslasuit* [2016-] uses an electro-tactile haptic feedback system to allow tracking of articular body movements and synchronize entirely with its avatar.

VR therefore takes the concept of *dwelling* in an opposite direction. If the techniques of ritual possession deprive a shaman's body of its independence (Cohen 2008, 246–47), and he becomes the physical habitat of a spirit, the disembodied consciousness of the VR player submerges him in an artificially replicated body in imagined space. As the *posthuman*, referred to as a 'cyborg manifesto' eroding the boundary between machine and organism (Haraway [1985] 2016, 5), is defined as *"a coupling so intense and multifaceted,"* where *"the biological organism"* and *"the informational circuits in which the organism is enmeshed"* are indistinguishable (Hayles 1999, 35), the body, formerly subordinated to spirit, becomes a catalytic agent or even *imago dei* creator of its virtual self.

According to Frazer, this idea of *"god incarnated in human form"* was an early alternative apparent in religious history of the man-god notion *"in which gods and men are still viewed as beings of much the same order"* (Frazer 1929, 92). By contrast, in the humanoid of virtuality armed with Artificial Intelligence, we see the superhuman retrieving his title by going back to men *"before they are divided by the impassable gulf,"* maybe indeed thanks to all those human inventions which made the impassable passable.

After all performances, the shaman regains his own consciousness and comes down from the *Jack-dou* platform. Just as his limbs have been protected by spirits from the sharpened blades, so the VR user himself invests his avatar, receiving no physical injury despite the fierce battle raging in virtuality.

Here, regarding the symmetrical positions of spirituality and virtuality in a *dwelling perspective*, we even find converse patterns of translocation regarding evolutionary beings in nomadic nature between worlds, through the technique or metaphor of embodiment: a spiritual being penetrates a physical body, and *vice-versa* this physicality embodies the virtual avatar. Does it demonstrate world expansion through imagination, or does it imply repeatedly hierarchical reincarnations of an evolutionary being, from the god-spirit, through humankind, to an autonomous virtual creature? Wherever the truth may be found, it seems clear that man places himself as the core subject of those three worlds, as a quasi-divine liberal mediator who can change his state of beingness, by using reproduced mediating tools. Thus, the mode of human presence in a digital era cosmology seems to have inherited both visions: the exploratory spirit of earlier centuries and a 'neo-shamanic' concept of incarnation are thus condensed in a single gadget. Then, how do both world views—expansive or convergent with respect to immaterial environments—allow *homo deus* to persist in their extended world?

II.

What makes the *séjour* longer? Traditional cosmology, comprising the notion of a spiritual world, gives us a hint in the notion of "belief" for a second such condition of *dwelling* in immateriality. Convictions, anchored in personal experience of mystic phenomena and its cultural transmission, certainly fertilized the formation and persistence of a contour-less universe.

What we see in the scenographic context of ritual performance would fit Geertz's analysis of religion: "*A system of symbols which acts to establish powerful, pervasive and long-lasting moods and motivations in men by formulating conceptions of a general order of existence, and clothing these conceptions with such an aura of factuality that the moods and motivations seem uniquely realistic*" (Geertz 1973, 91–119). Although anthropology will never offer any clear convictions as to the truth or not of spiritual phenomena or religion (Bharati 1971, 231), and since it's been a relatively short period that technology has emerged as a new foundation for belief systems (Lewis 2003, 659–61), it seems that shamanic ritual and VR technology ultimately find their convergence on utopian ideals in a common aim "*to be realistic.*"

Whether relying on tailored systems or not, enticing a person's belief seems therefore to be essential for the "realistic" persistence of these worlds that semantically signify *dwelling* for a digital humanity. Naturally, the technique and technology of both ritual and VR tools involve the formation of belief, engaging supernatural or sensorial verisimilitude.

Sperber categorizes belief as factual or representational (Sperber 1982, 74), comparable to Van Leeuwen's division between factual and religious credence (Van Leeuwen 2014, 698–99). While factual beliefs are "*simply things we know,*" representational beliefs correspond to what are called "*beliefs, opinions or convictions,*" mostly of mental representation. Nevertheless, both can be co-present in one circumstance and also considered "*apparently irrational belief*" with respect to each other, in factual or symbolist approach (Sperber 1982, 149–80).

To give here an example, the ritual mask predicates belief through its two faces—obverse and reverse sides—with both performers and spectators as third parties. The mask wearer would go into trance and spectators observe what is happening. Both start with factual belief in perceived facts—the sensorial feeling of mask wearer through performance, and visual observation by the spectators. But sooner or later, that belief tends to revert to the representational, solicited in a religious perspective (e.g., I felt wind = spirit came to me). This composite of two different characters of belief can collide in a person's mind causing a confusion. It may generate *"disbelief in belief,"* that Van Leeuwen finds in religious credence, manifest in imaginative play such as ritual performance (Boudry and Coyne 2016, 6).

Then what does the "act of believing" mean in virtual reality, causing "disbelief in belief?" In most VR contents, the designed "state of immersion" comes after acquaintance with an interactive structure between contrived representations (avatar, objects, structures, path, etc.) and actions required of the player (Sedig and Parsons 2013, 85–8). User consciousness starts to conduct tasks using stored factual beliefs as data-base to interpret symbols (e.g., monsters are enemies) (Sperber 1997, 68). Once accustomed, it continues with automatism (e.g., use fist to hit monster) in a range of symbols, also uniquely realistic to consciousness, where the confusion may begin.

Another episode demonstrates that the evolved technology can sprout belief in such disbelief : In 2019, I met the developer of re-educative VR therapy contents in collaboration with a university hospital in South Korea where, due to cerebrovascular accident (CVA), patients with hemiparalysis are practicing with VR games.[16] Contents consist of playful exercises such as hammering or catching a ball, obliging patients to move upper limbs for the task. Such simulation is not photorealistic, but once absorbed a patient's brain overlaps the scene and appropriates those simulated graphic hands as their own. These optical illusions are based on motor imagery (MI) that involves activation of the neural system while a person imagines performing a task or moving the body without physically performing the movement. The principle of mirror therapy (MT), a well-known example of MI, demonstrates the effects of an image perceived in the mirror, and shows the ability of vision to be so misleading as to be restorative of cerebral function [Image 4].[17]

---

16   Interview in Dong-guk University Hospital, 2019.

17   MT is often used for one paralyzed or amputated limb when the other remains normally functional. Placing a mirror box between legs or arms, one reflects the image of the healthy limb. Seeing the reflection of his healthy leg, the person enjoys an illusory perception, as if the damaged leg is functioning.

Image 4: A cerebral scan that shows plasticity of the brain: a zone activated by robotic re-education is coloured in red. (Image source: www.materic.or.k r)

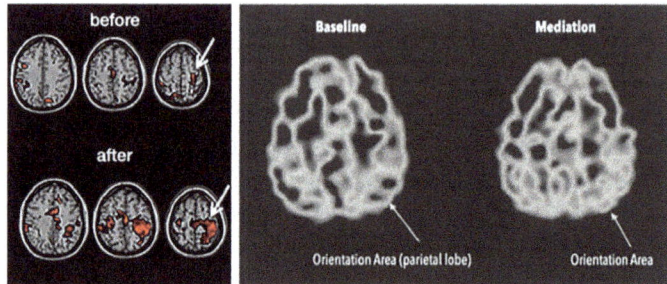

Such that, with the simple task of catching a ball, a single user in their first-person optical perspective can throw it or catch it using hand controls, synchronized with graphic VR limbs. While playing, the sight of a ball coming suddenly towards the user induces an unconditional reflex of instant illusion. Patients are fully aware of their hemiparalysis, but the optical stimulus of the visual hands and ball coming towards them generate a new and momentary belief: forgetting their physical disability they try to catch it by hand, and surprisingly, such brain-deception activates the regeneration of nerves. In just a few years of such therapeutic practices, VR was justified as being effective on brain plasticity and restoring damaged brain parts (Lee et al. 2019, 258–61).[18]

Even so, the momentary "belief" activated by virtuality, that we might call an "illusion," is not regarded as possessing the same quality of "belief" as that generated by cerebral stimulus interacting with our conscious mind, which "disbelieves" the realness of VR and considers VR experience only as a therapeutic tool, not a real event.

While ritual objects or VR tools are not intrinsically objects of belief but remain mediators, the efficacy of both nevertheless establishes each belief system. The only difference, in technology and science, would be that such accumulated beliefs establish their own with verifiable criteria, open to testing (Eddy 2004, 53–4). That system can even serve as another ritual tool, in the sense that our interviewee evoked: "I think God is using me through [VR]..., I'm only a tool."

On this discordance between beliefs regarding what is real, we nevertheless find directions branching out by way of demonstration, which attempt to adduce ontological evidence of two endemic realisms. Simply put, shamanic ritual strives to

---

18   Brain plasticity refers to a capacity of neuronal brain cells to restore a damaged part. When stimulated at a certain level, the neuronal cells around it will replace the role of the damaged part.

overcome the laws of physics—inasmuch as the shaman showed us his bare feet un-wounded after his performance on the Jack-dou—whilst VR technology takes an op-posite direction, aiming to duplicate attributes of physicality in virtuality.

Corporeal boundaries of individual and society

We must reckon then, with *what individuals and society experience in belief of an extended reality*, since establishing one's belief system on an invisible world is bound to condi-tion any subordinated taxonomy of beliefs, such as world view, paradigm, or model of reality (Eddy 2004, 53).

Through numerous supernatural phenomena, a shaman's lifeworld range seems to embrace spiritual reality as *fait accompli*. To our question on the eventuality of quit-ting his profession, our interviewee answered in firm manner with a belief common to shamanic culture: "*There'll be misfortune, to me and also to my family, we can even die. It's the spiritual punishment one can never know.*" As Geertz points out regarding the matter of suffering as a religious problem, we learn "*paradoxically, not how to avoid suffering but how to suffer*" or how to make bearable, supportable and sufferable (Geertz 1973, 104). The shaman's belief in the spirit-possession of his body, potentially implicat-ing misfortune, predicates another system with which to treat his fate (Perrin 2017, 88). His life relies on punishment feedback, such as limited life choices, just as VR gamers follow positive and negative feedback loops to determine the final outcome.

Image 5: An overview of South Koreans' general conceptions, regarding lifeworld ranges and their geography, illustrated schematically. (Diagram by author.)

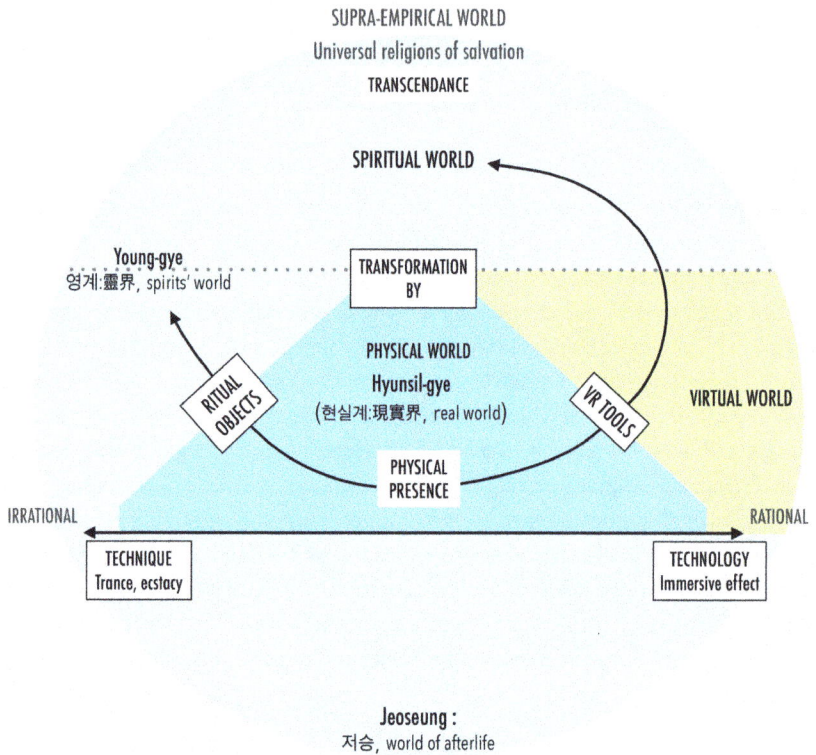

In a broader view, confrontations between religion and science, tradition and modernism, are surely worldwide phenomena. Presented as "riding tools," these semantic excursions into parallel environments combine the two, revealing a paradoxical phase at work in South Korea.

It is observed, in a schematized concept of lifeworld ranges in traditional cosmology, that the spiritual world [영계:靈界: *young-gye*] is distinguished from the afterlife [저승: *jeoseung*], and disposed on a higher or same level as the physical world [현실계:現實界][Image 5].[19]

Even though traditional outlooks—shamanist and Confucianist—are considered officially obsolete, they are still strongly central to those upper and lower

---

19   Conceptual geography of the spiritual world has complex features. The Upper level would show them identical in Christianity or Buddhism, defined as religions of universal salvation by Karl Jasper. Meanwhile, the mixed position in parallel or on a higher level can be seen in the appellation of *chun-ji-sin-myoung*, which signifies the god of sky and of earth.

worlds. Within a fatalistic conception of the human condition, shamanism subsists by way of reasoning on causality. On the other hand, Confucianism still seems to govern the social system in physical reality, with hierarchical classification according to gender, seniority, as still revealed in parental, social, and professional relationships (Kister 1997, 35).

On this basis, a technological innovation of *Extended Reality* (XR) is changing the conceptual plan of an immaterial world, infiltrating the sphere of spirits by man-made artefact.[20] During the pandemic period some Korean Protestant churches initiated VR online Sunday worship, and the number of participants has continuously increased since 2021. On the other hand a female shaman, designated as intangible cultural asset by the *Hwang-hae-do* region, recently reproduced her ritual performance of *Man-gu-dae-tak* [만구대탁:萬口大擇] as VR content, accessible by VR headset.

Image 6: In South Korea, a shaman riding Jack-dou blades compares with VR players surfing on VR boards. (Photos by author.)[21]

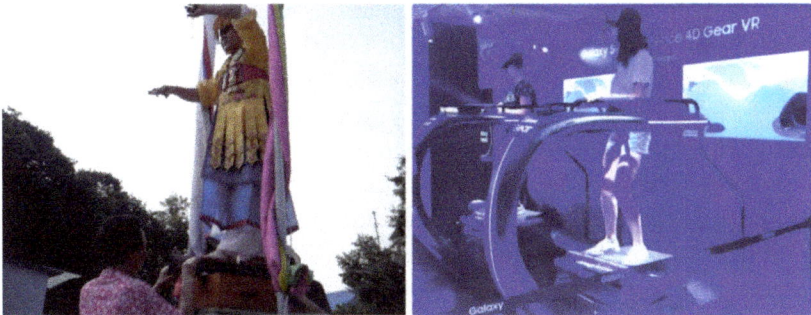

Progress in technology and capitalistic success abetting, opposing such technological ascension to the shamanic idea of a spiritual world should be somewhat ontologically and ideologically ironic for Koreans. By sustaining its adherents' practical aim—prosperity in a mundane lifeworld—Korean shamanism has been able to survive until now, [22] with considerable cultural influence on the general religious

---

20   Extended Reality (XR) refers to all environments combining physical and virtual functions generating human-machine interactions through digital technology.

21   Images extracted from field research report video [https://jyeon.com/2020/12/28/2197/].

22   Korean shamanism went into a downward trend since the nation adopted Buddhism as its national religion in the 4th century. After losing its political function at the end of the Goryeo dynasty, the banishment of shamanism was initiated. From the 16th century, the Joseon dynasty, established on Confucian ideas, continued expulsion of shamanism, especially through the neo-Confucian faction of philosophical lineage called Sarim [사림파:士林派]. Shamanism even lost its social position, but retained adepts for personal consultation un-

mind-set of Koreans, even those of other confessions: yet maintaining the pursuit of earthly prosperity, and mystic empiricism. On the other hand, recent technological progress and productivity may find their roots in the « *Silhak* (실학: 實學, practical studies) » fraction of 17th century neo-Confucian lineage, doubtless opposed to shamanic ideas. Considering this background, the use of technological tools to re-vive consciousness of a spiritual world reveals a compromising encounter between two ideological counterparts. While rationalist and scientific thought informs the glazed surfaces of skyscrapers, projecting that new image of the country, the in-dividuals sitting at their desks oscillate consciously or unconsciously in the face of these residual survivals of the past: superstitious thought and futuristic-oriented goals in dominant hierarchical relations which, seen from the outside, pass for ir-rational and contradictory to their perceived image. Surfing on VR boards in a *VR Experience Store*, they might hardly recall *Jack-dou* blades, on which shamans perform the ritual elsewhere in the same peninsula [Image 6].

This reveals a polymorph mode of human being, incubated in multiform sur-roundings, fashioned by vestiges of their shamanic tradition, in a Confucianist-dominated culture, under technology-oriented social policy (Seo et al. 2011, 33). It neatly explains the progressive switch of values from the polytheism of shamanic spiritualism, through Confucianist atheism, to the technocratic scientism of *homo deus*.

Back to the rashly drawn conceptual world map [Image 1], how should we cope with this co-habitation of apparently incompatible ideologies? The *metapattern* con-struct, used *"in the Batesonian spirit"* as biological scientist Tyler Volk confesses, could provide evidence for the parallelism of three realms. Bateson's actual term seeks *"pat-tern of pattern"* (Bateson 1979, 16).[23] Ritual objects and VR tools may help only to dis-cover the latent *metapattern* which would link those conceptual constructions of im-material space. There, an axis, or absolute standard of one's experience of presence is no more limited to materiality, or tools positioned at the core of indispensable context-making processes, than our preconceptions of tools in the physical environ-ment, rather auxiliary and subordinated. Here, our *god-human* regards tools as ve-hicles for transcendence, driving back and forth the semantic conversion of spatial self-context from here to there, from physical reality to an immaterial one.

---

til now. Scholars find the reason in the fact that it is the only religion claiming prosperity in the mundane lifeworld, whilst Confucian ideas criticized shaman ritual as unreasonable, wi-cked, treacherous and futile [cf. Sejong-sillok, 1426, see bibliography]. Nevertheless, Korean Confucianism met with a second ideological collision, initially "Silhak faction [실학 : 實學, practical studies]" from the 17th century, and latterly with present generation rationalism, which favors productivity and technological progress.

23   The meta pattern can be understood as an art of bilateral symmetry, which connects crab to lobster, our hands to a crab's claws, between brassica or all living creatures, as a base plan which is "so wide-flung that it appears throughout the spectrum of reality."

The validity of such 'dereistic' reasoning, which may seem overly speculative, hinges inevitably on how and in which perspective we examine them. Those two worlds, seemingly in diametrical opposition, co-exist however in our society, expanding the apparent borderline of a perceived world, as conceptual model structure of what *homo deus* calls a hyperphysical scene of *reality*, where the *self* may play the leading role behind his social *persona* (Turner 1987, 145). As such it becomes the new mappa mundi for "those who believe," a represented space where we oscillate between habitual loops of discomfort and relocation, to settle down and assert our volatile presence.

Conclusion

> "The true 'spatial revolution' of the twentieth century is the explication of the human sojourn or residence in an interior via the dwelling machine, climate design and environmental planning, but also... cosmic space and virtual space." (Sloterdijk 2016, 469)

On a vast meadow in Mongolia, I vaguely remember that, instead of using a fixed post, a dog's leg was folded at the knee and tied up with a string, to ensure that the animal didn't escape. Such direct means of bondage shatter a quadruped's equilibrium and make it think of nothing else than lying down on the grass, gravity-bound. Bodies are obviously vulnerable to tools, even to a such tiny string, no doubt to any 'dwelling machine,' that determines their scope of possibilities.

The conceptual birth of two worlds, spiritual and virtual, without matter and without gravity, would then be a real uprising against physical restriction. Likewise, the separation of human spirit from body would have been first to trigger this projection of a second world. Nevertheless, in our reality extended by the latest technologies, we discover more active trials of reconciliation with the body, and much radical intervention through tools. Body, considered as passive host to spirits, is kindly invited to recover its forgotten rights to 'dwell' in its virtual host, as learnt undoubtedly from former guests. In this excursion, surpassing three worlds, humans may lose their place as creator, but are connected as links in a chain of 'tools.'

This paper is no hypothesis of existentialist philosophical perspective, concerned with the threat or favour of technology, sometimes inclined to "engulf its creators" (Feenberg 2004, 12–3), nor does it make pretense of rigorously scientific or theoretical conclusions. Rather, its proposition is to re-view through a poly-scope a new origin of species, an era where our neo-biosphere is defined via such animation of inert objects, and ponder over further genesis, in a chapter where multi-substantial organisms attempt co-presence. However ambitious the title, what remains vividly captured in my brain is individual interlocutors' testimony, and how they framed their lives in fusion with such tools as "belief generators." Beyond the purpose of my thesis,[24] I believe that these testimonies merit commitment to record, as the valid basis of all source-related and discipline-based extrapolation. Just as with the leg-bound dog, humans are aware of an incapacity to release ourselves from our built reality, and wherever we celebrate the art of tie-up in another firm belief, we call upon our tools.

Bibliography

Anonymous. "AI in Virtual Reality." *The New Frontier of Intelligent Reality (IR)*. IEEE International Conference of Intelligent Reality (2022) https://digitalreality.ieee.or g/publications/ai-in-virtual-reality.

Anonymous. *Sejong-Sillok, The Veritable Records of King Sejong*, Vol. 34, 8th year. 7th Nov. 1426.

Bateson, Gregory. *La nature et la pensée*. Paris: Seuil, 1979.

Bharati, Agehananda. "Anthropological Approaches to the Study of Religion: Ritual and Belief Systems." *Biennial Review of Anthropology* 7 (1971): 230–82.

Boudry, Maarten and Jerry Coyne. "Disbelief in belief: On the cognitive status of supernatural beliefs." *Philosophical Psychology* (2016): 1–15.

Brandstetter, Gabriele. "Ritual as Scene and Discourse: Art and Science Around 1990 as exemplified by *Le Sacre du printemps*." *The World of Music* 40, no. 1 (1998): 37–59.

Cahen, Olivier. *L'image en relief*. Paris: Masson. 1989.

Cipresso, Pietro and Giuseppe Riva. "Virtual Reality for Artificial Intelligence: human-centred simulation for social science." *Annual Review of Cybertheraphy and Telemedicine*. Ed. Brenda Wiederhold, Giuseppe Riva and Mark Wiederhold. Amsterdam: IOS Press, 2015: 177–81.

Cohen, Emma, and Justin L. Barrett. "Conceptualizing Spirit Possession: Ethnographic and Experimental Evidence." *Ethos* 36, no. 2 (2008): 246–267.

Denègre, Jean. *Sémiologie et conception cartographique*. Paris: Hermès Science, 2005.

Descola, Philippe and Tim Ingold. *Être au monde. Quelle expérience commune?* Lyon: Presses Universitaires de Lyon, 2014.

Eddy, Bob. "On Belief Systems," *ETC: A Review of General Semantics* 61, no. 1 (2004): 51–56.

---

24   Doctoral research on *Changement de perspectives du monde réel et connexité avec les objets-outils*, from 2016 to 2022 at EHESS, Paris.

Ehrsson, H. Henrik. "The concept of body ownership and its relation to multisensory integration." *The New Handbook of Multisensory Processes*. Ed. Barry E. Stein. Cambridge: MIT Press, 2012: 775–92.

Etzioni, Amitai. "Toward a Theory of Public Ritual." *Sociological Theory* 18, no. 1 (2000): 44–59.

Feenberg, Andrew. *(Re)penser la technique: vers une technologie démocratique*. Trans. Anne-Marie Dibon. Paris: La Découverte, 2004.

Frazer, James. *The Golden Bough: a study in magic and religion*. London: Macmillan & Co., 1929.

Frazer, James. *The New Golden Bough*. Ed. Theodor H. Gaster. New York: S. G. Phillips, 1959.

Geertz, Clifford. "Religion as a cultural system." *The Interpretation of Cultures*. New York: Basic Books Inc. Publishers,1966: 87–125.

Goffman, Erving. *An Essay on the Organization of Experience*. New York: Harper & Row, 1974.

Goodman, Nelson. *Manières de faire des mondes* (1978). Trans. Marie-Dominique Popelard. Paris: Jacqueline Chambon, 1992.

Haraway, Donna. "A Cyborg Manifesto: Science, Technology, and Socialist-Feminism in the Late Twentieth Century" (1985). *Manifestly Haraway*. Minneapolis and London: University of Minnesota Press, 2016.

Hayles, N. Katherine. *How we became Posthuman: Virtual bodies in Cybernetics, Literature, and Informatics*. Chicago: University of Chicago Press, 1999.

Husserl, Edmund. *Ideas Pertaining to a Pure Phenomenology and to a Phenomenological Philosophy / Second book / Studies in the Phenomenology of Constitution*. Trans. Richard Rojcewicz and André Schuwer. Dordrecht: Kluwer Academic Publishers, 1989.

Ingold, Tim. *The Perception of the Environment: Essays on Livelihood, Dwelling and Skill*. New York: Routledge, 2000.

Kelekna, Pita. *The Horse in Human History*. New York: Cambridge University Press, 2009.

Kister, Daniel A. *Korean shamanist ritual: symbols and dramas of transformation*. Budapest: Akadémiai Kiadé, 1997.

Knottnerus, J. David. "Collective Events, Rituals, and Emotions." *Advances in Group Processes* 27. Ed. Shane R. Thye and Edward J. Lawler. Bingley: Emerald Group Publishing Ltd., 2010: 39–61.

Latour, Bruno. *Où suis-je? Leçons du confinement à l'usage des terrestres*. Paris: Empêcheurs De Penser En Rond, 2021.

Lee, Seung Hak, Jung, Hae Yoon, Yun, Seo Jung, Oh, Byung Mo and Han Gil Seo. "Upper Extremity Rehabilitation Using Fully Immersive Virtual Reality Games With a Head Mount Display: A Feasibility Study." *PM&R* 12, no. 3 (2019): 257–262.

Leroi-Gourhan, André. *Le geste et la parole: La mémoire et les rythmes*. Paris: Albin Michel, 1965.

Leroi-Gourhan, André. *Milieu et techniques: évolution et techniques*. Paris: Albin Michel, 1945.

Lewis, William, Agarwal, Ritu, and V. Sambamurthy. "Sources of Influence on Beliefs about Information Technology Use: An Empirical Study of Knowledge Workers." *MIS Quarterly* 27, no. 4 (2003): 657–78.

Lotman, Iouri (Jurij M.). *La structure du texte artistique* (1970). Trans. Anne Fournier. Paris: Gallimard, 1973.

Malik, Aditya. "The swirl of worlds: possession, porosity and embodiment," *Religious Individualisation: Historical Dimensions and Comparative Perspectives*. Ed. Martin Fuchs, Antje Linkenbach, Martin Mulsow, Bernd-Christian Otto, Rahul Bjørn Parson and Jörg Rüpke. Berlin, Boston: De Gruyter, 2020: 559–582.

Mauss, Marcel. "Une Catégorie de L'Esprit Humain: La Notion de Personne Celle de Moi." *The Journal of the Royal Anthropological Institute of Great Britain and Ireland* 68 (1938).

Merrill, Michael S. "Masks, Metaphor and Transformation: The Communication of Belief in Ritual Performance." *Journal of Ritual Studies* 18, no. 1 (2004): 16–33.

Mitcham, Carl. *Thinking Through Technology: The Path Between Engineering and Philosophy*. Chicago: University of Chicago Press,1994.

Murray Craig D., and Sixsmith, Judith. "The Corporeal Body in Virtual Reality." *Ethos* 27, no. 3 (1999): 315–343.

Pavis, Patrice. *L'Analyse des Spectacles*. Domont: Armand Colin, 2008.

Pernet, Henry. *Ritual Masks: Deceptions and Revelations*. Columbia, SC: University of South Carolina Press, 1992.

Perrin, Michel. *Le chamanisme*. Paris: Presses Universitaires de France, 2017.

Pier, John. "Monde narratif et sémiosphère." *Communications* 103, no. 2 (2018): 265–86.

Plato, *Œuvres complètes. Tome VII, 1ère partie: La République, Livres IV-VII*. Trans. Émile Chambry. Paris: Les Belles Lettres, 1933.

Reed, Daniel B. *Dan Ge Performance: Masks and Music in Contemporary Côte d'Ivoire*. Indiana: Indiana University Press, 2003.

Rooney, Anne. *Cartes chroniques du monde connu*. Trans. Mathieu Auverdin and Sarah Grassart. Paris: Chronique Edition, 2018.

Sedig, Kamran. "Need for a Prescriptive Taxonomy of Interaction for Mathematical Cognitive Tools." *Computational Science -ICCS: Lecture Notes in Computer Science* 3038 (2004):1030-37. https://doi.org/10.1007/978-3-540-24688-6_133.

Sedig, Kamran, and Paul Parsons. "Interaction Design for Complex Cognitive Activities with Visual Representations: A Pattern-Based Approach." *AIS Transactions on Human-Computer Interaction* 5, no. 2 (2013): 84–133.

Seo, Young-Dae, Lee, Kyung-Yub, Lee, Yong-Bum, Heo, Yong-Ho, Hong, Tae-Han, and National Institute of Korean History. *Shamanism, Connection between God and Human*. Seoul: Kyungin Publishing, 2011.

Servier, Jean. *Les techniques de l'invisible*. Monaco: Editions du Rocher, 1994.

Sloterdijk, Peter. *Foams: Spheres III*. Cambridge: MIT Press, 2016.

Sperber, Dan. "Intuitive and Reflective Beliefs." *Mind and Language* 12, no. 1 (1997): 67–83.

Sperber, Dan. *Le savoir des anthropologues: trois essais*. Paris: Hermann, 1982.

Taussig, Michael. *Mimesis and Alterity: a Particular History of the Senses*. New York: Routledge, 1993.

Turner, Victor. *The Anthropology of Performance*. New York: PAJ Publication, 1987.

Van Leeuwen, Neil. "Religious credence is not factual belief." *Cognition* 133, no. 3 (2014): 698–99.

White, Michele. *The Body and the Screen: Theories of Internet Spectatorship*. Cambridge: MIT Press, 2006.

Yi, J. S., Kang, Y. A., Stasko J., and J. Jacko. "Toward a Deeper Understanding of the Role of Interaction in Information Visualization," *IEEE Transactions on Visualization and Computer Graphics* 13 (2007):1224-1231.

Virtual and Physical Ways of Being Present in Odissi Dance Networks in Bhubaneswar in India[1]

Barbara Čurda

Abstract *In this paper, I reflect on what presence is all about, leaning on personal experiences and my fieldwork in Bhubaneswar, capital of the Indian State of Odisha, from September 2021 onwards. The particular context of the COVID-19 pandemic has multiplied our encounters with disembodied modalities of presence. This poses the question of what differences it makes to engage with somebody's presence virtually or physically. While the fieldwork I undertook during this period was marked by the constraints to which both I and my research participants were subjected, forcing me to adapt my fieldwork, modifying the ways in which physical contact could be established, it also raised into prominence the differences that arose from an appraisal of virtual or physical presences of dance practitioners. I analyse these differences utilizing the particular example of my assessment of Odissi dance activity in the early 2020s in Bhubaneswar, based on both virtual sources and physical encounters with the material world. As I assess the perception of these presences, I show the relational nature of this phenomenon within a network of both human and non-human, living and non-living beings, as well as the different ways it engages the (human) perceiver in emotional and sensory manners.*

Keywords *presence; perception; imagination; embodiment; materiality; knowing*

Introduction

Pondicherry, 4th June 2023. I am packing my luggage, as I am about to travel. The room in which I am staying is situated on the ground floor, in the midst of dense greenery. As I shift my bag from one spot on the floor to another, I hear a little sound,

---

1   This article is part of a project that has received funding from the Eurpean Union's Horizon 2020 research and innovation programme under the Marie Skłodowska-Curie grant agreement No 101033051.

as if something has fallen or jumped onto the ground. Something that has this capacity to adhere to surfaces and is slightly sticky. It is the quality of sound I hear that makes me think so. Intrigued, I look beneath the bag. Nothing seems to be there. But I thought I saw a glimpse of a little animal. A lizard?

The kind of sensory experience I encountered makes me feel that the sound is somewhat different from the one I am used to from lizards when they let themselves fall from the walls. Yet, as nothing is detected, I forget the episode.

Sometime later, my eyes wander across the floor and focus on a spot about one meter from where this happened. A small scorpion is positioned on the ground, its tail curved, pointing upwards, ready to attack. Is that the 'thing' I encountered? I suppose so.

A kind of a puzzle is comprised in this story. A puzzle about a little animal being present in the room, but not being present to my perception. But, wait? Did not some of my senses capture something about this presence, while others did not? Indeed, in the first part of this experience, I perceived a presence through the sound it made. In the second, it was through my eyesight. Each time, I arrived at preliminary conclusions, based on the perceptions generated by this small event. It is interesting that I was subconsciously aware that this particular presence – of a thing or animal – required my attention. However, it is only upon viewing the animal with my eyes that I became able to consider the danger that existed in the situation. Each way of perceiving this presence made me aware of an aspect of it. I realize that many other beings may be present around me which I am not able to perceive – beings whose impact on my life may be irrelevant or, as in this particular case, potentially quite disruptive. Their presence, whether I acknowledge it or not, contributes to the life and happenings in this room. The specific ways in which I engage with them, intentionally or not, make a clear difference. And they actually constitute context-specific ways of exploring my surroundings and gaining knowledge about them.

This indicates that presence requires urgent attention in the contemporary world. For, as formulated by Eberhard Wolff and Sebastian Dümling on the occasion of the conference panel *Being there – but how? On the transformation of presences,* held at the EASA 2022 conference, presence "now can be physical, face-to-face, digital, distant, online, virtual, contactless, personal, in person, in vivo, usual, real, home, offline, sensual, etc.[2]". Presence, therefore, seems to have become something more complex than the phenomena described above. Or maybe not? In order to shed some light on this intriguing topic, it is this question of the influence that our ways of engaging with particular presences exert on what we know, or may potentially get to know, which I would like to explore in the following pages. How do we human beings gather knowledge on the world around us through encounters with diverse

---

2   Please see the full abstract of the conference panel here: https://nomadit.co.uk/conference/easa2022/p/11346 .

modalities of presence? What differences does it make that some presences may be physical and others not? Do we assess them in the same ways? Is there a change? And if there is, then what is it about? Furthermore, what effects does it have?

Regarding exploring this question, I would like, in the following pages, to take the readers on a journey through my encounters with presence during the fieldwork I undertook in Bhubaneswar, capital city of the State of Odisha in India, from September 2021 onwards. This city is the centre of a very dynamic activity in the field of Odissi dance, a practice considered to be one of the "Indian classical dances".[3] By using the example of the practices of this dance, I will examine the influence of different modalities of presence on our ways of knowing. The example of Odissi dance in Bhubaneswar lends itself particularly well to this analysis, as the fieldwork I am going to use in the discussion took place in the context of the sanitary crisis, and this generated quite a few reflections on presence. Many have experienced the tensions the pandemic triggered in academic fields in which direct human contact is required to work. As the tension continued, it appeared to numerous people that it would never be possible again to undertake fieldwork as before. I was also affected by this situation: in spring 2021, as I was preparing to leave for India in the midst of the pandemic, the great Delta COVID wave, the one that caused a spectacular death rate and made headlines in the news worldwide from April onwards, raised doubts on whether I could start my research project as planned in July of the same year.[4] I faced all sorts of comments, and amongst others, some suggested that I could start my research from France, using the Internet as my first tool for investigation. This idea appeared somewhat strange to me: How could I do serious ethnographic research about individuals, their lives and surroundings, without being present on the spot, as had been dictated by Bronislaw Malinowsky (1922)?

The great Delta wave subsided, and by September 2021, I had started fieldwork in Bhubaneswar. However, the context continued to be strongly altered by the sanitary crisis, and this added suspense to my endeavour: Firstly, because, although figures were not acute in India at that time, it had required me to undertake special procedures to obtain permission to start my fieldwork. I was committed to conduct it with due respect of sanitary protocols. In other words, the ways in which I could make myself present amongst my potential research participants were circumscribed. And secondly, because the pandemic impacted what was being researched: In which manners would dance practitioners[5] turn out to be present at a time

---

3   For information on the "classical" genre in the fields of music and dance in India, see, for
      example, Subramanian (2006).
4   These questions raised diverse administrative issues because my project, GATRODI, had ob-
      tained funding from the European Commission.
5   I use the term "practitioner" in order to designate any person engaged with dance activity
      in a practice-oriented manner. This includes, of course, dancers, dance teachers, people who

when ordinary primary educational institutions were still closed in Odisha, when secondary schools were only partly open, and left parents with the choice of either sending their children physically to their schools or letting them partake in online classes? In this anxiety-driven context, dance schools were most likely to be closed, presences were very likely to be, to a great extent, disembodied, the ways in which I could be present with dance practitioners, constricted. Let me, therefore, get back to the puzzle about the little scorpion – which suggests that it does not require any sanitary crisis for presence to appear as a complex phenomenon. Indeed, long before encounters between human beings started taking place in virtual conferences, the phenomenon of presence had attracted a lot of attention in the field of philosophy. Philosopher Alva Noë discusses a phenomenon that is related to my experience described above in his article "Experience of the world in time" (2006), leaning on a well-known debate on the topic of presence by Husserl: The example he uses is that of a tomato that, despite being present, cannot be seen simultaneously by a person from all its sides. Thereby, he draws the attention towards a fundamental problem of presence: the tomato may exist physically in a space of which a part is discernible to some of my senses, however, whatever I do, I will not be able, at a given point of time, from a specific location in space, to verify its presence with all of my senses,[6] as a whole – and not simply as a slice of a tomato. Yet, Noë asserts that an individual has "a sense of the presence of the object as a whole" (2006, 26).

This disposition, which concerns the ways in which we are functioning on a cognitive plane, opens up a great variety of questions regarding presence. Particularly, it clearly demonstrates that presence forcefully raises interrogations on its appraisement. For what is presence if it cannot be assessed by an entity that can, in whichever way, make some kind of declaration asserting that the object or living being in question is present? This is important: As a matter of fact, if nobody perceives the presence of the tomato (or any other thing, person), it (or they) may actually be assumed to be absent. And as the example of the unnoticed presence of the scorpion shows, the perception of absence does not preclude any effects of the present being – even acute ones. On the other hand, it is possible to perceive the presence of an object or a person which/who may be physically absent, and, therefore, assume that it, he or she is present. Noë states that "[t]he world is present, in perception, not by being present (e.g., represented depicted) in consciousness all at once, as it were, but by being available all at once to the skillful perceiver" (2005, 243). On behalf of these remarks, it is possible to say that, regardless of whether presences may be embodied

---

view themselves as both interpreters and transmitters of the dance, and many others, such as journalists and art lovers.

6   Noë pays quite a bit of attention to analysing through which means we perceive – a point which I cannot elaborate on here. For details, please consult his article.

or even real, they are actually active: When they are perceived, they trigger a variety of responses in the perceiver. And when they are not perceived, they still have an effect on people's lives. Let me, therefore, get back to my case example.

I acknowledge that Odissi dance practitioners are present both in virtual and physical manners: in discourses, in geographical spaces and on websites. It appears relevant to inspect these presences as well as others as, according to Layton, "our mind becomes manifest in the objects, traces, and leavings that we generate during our lifetime" (2003, 458). Accordingly, in the following inquiry, I will first direct my attention towards modalities of presence of Odissi in collective imagination. I will, therefore, expose some of the ways in which the practices of these dances are, or become, easily available in people's minds through common representations or by being advertised, for example, on websites. I will then concentrate on the manners in which presences of Odissi practitioners became manifest to me during my investigations, as I was, in my quest for truth, trying to cut through common sense constructions in order to assess the phenomenon of Odissi dance activity by looking at both disembodied and embodied modalities of their presences. Finally, I wish to reserve some space in this discussion to reflect upon the differences between the modalities of presence described and the ways in which this shapes our actions and reactions.

Disembodied presences and the question of truth

While it is not possible here to engage in an intricate theoretical discussion on this subject, it is appropriate to state that societies continuously generate imaginary constructions, and one thing these do is influence their functioning – and sometimes in manners that maintain and reproduce power relations. To underscore the importance of such processes, I would like to remind readers that Durkheim treats social facts as things (1895). However 'unreal' they may be in the sense that they are deprived of any corporeal existence, their presence exists in people's minds. It is, therefore, important to document how this happens, and identify at least some of the particular processes at work in relation to this.

Presence of the dance in imagination

Many individuals are actually aware that the disembodiment of social life described above in connection with the COVID-19 pandemic is only the enhancement of an already existing, commonly known phenomenon: Long before the advent of the Internet, presences have always been partly 'virtual', in the sense that they belong to the realm of imagination. Noë states that "[p]erception is the encounter with the world from a point of view" (2005, 243), and this, I hold, need not be the physical world.

I even advocate that what is perceived does not actually need to exist. In point of fact, we are used to encountering the presences of entities or beings, the existence of which we cannot verify. Take the example of ghosts: The answer to the question whether they actually exist may be different according to the cultural backgrounds in which it is taken up. Yet, independently of what the answer is and of the fact that such an answer may hold 'true' or not, some individuals feel the presences of ghosts and are affected by them.

It is not my purpose here to take any stance on how 'real' or 'fake' these presences may be, and whether these experiences should be tagged as "hallucinatory" rather than "perceptive" (Noë 2005, 254). It is sufficient for this inquiry to concentrate on their effect on individuals and groups of individuals, because "the occurrence of a distinct kind of state of consciousness – hallucinatory consciousness – [...] is such that we can be unable to tell it apart from the genuinely perceptual state" (Noë 2005, 254). This is not true only for hallucinations, because phenomena that, in diverse ways, may be considered 'unreal' or 'inexistent' populate our existences in multiple ways. Social sciences have underscored for a long time that things do not need to 'be real' to generate 'real' effects on people's lives. This has been amply documented by social theorists. To cite an example out of my own research experience, in the 1990s, Odissi dancers, masters and musicians of the dance anticipated that female practitioners of the dance would, once they married, not be allowed by their in-laws to pursue their dance activity. This had consequences on the ways in which male dance masters would engage with their female disciples, as they would not include them in their long-term career strategies. In turn, women who did not face the expected opposition by their in-laws, and were actually able to continue their dance activity after marriage, encountered resistance on the part of their male colleagues: their capacity to act (Giddens 1984) was impaired by the common anticipation that they would not be able to be long-term participants in the development of the dance.[7]

Jacques Pouchepadass reminds us that "to represent the other, is to manipulate him" (or her) (2000, 172). Representations, as we know, take many forms, some of which have a large-scale outreach, as the work *Orientalism* by Edward W. Said (1978) has amply documented. In the case of the dance form Odissi, powerful imaginary constructions present the dance as "an alluring and mysterious art, situated in ancient Orissan temples through a myth sustained by archaeological narratives" (Lopez Y Royo 2007, 159). Such discursive constructions make it appear as something very shiny, and associate its practices with the highest strata of society. It is not my purpose here, though it is worth exploring the subject, to analyse how such antiquity discourses have been thriving or often been linked to nationalism in some historic contexts. Let me, however, remind readers that, as Susan A. Reed points out, "[s]ince

---

7   This example reminds us of the theoretical proposition by Robert K. Merton (1948), who considers that anticipation plays a role in the production of social dynamics.

the late nineteenth and early twentieth centuries, with the rise of cultural nation-alisms in Europe and its colonies, dance has figured prominently in the creation of many ethnic and national 'cultures'" (2010, 5). Regarding the Indian case, Odissi and its representation as an inheritance of an antique practice holding a high cultural status concerns a whole group of dance and music practices belonging to the In-dian "classical" genre. Several authors have documented the emergence of this genre during the twentieth century in the context of rising Indian nationalism striving to free the country from colonial rule (e.g. Erdman 1996; Fratagnoli 2010; Gaston 1996; Leucci 2008; Shah 2002; Soneji 2012; Subramanian 2006; and for the specific case of Odissi: Carli 2000; Čurda 2013; Rodier 2004; Schnepel 2005[8]). Yet, the common rep-resentation of the associated practices as being 'antique', despite the abundance of work unearthing their status as reinvented traditions (Hobsbawm and Ranger 1983) and being designated by some researchers to be a "modern myth of ancient heritage" (Erdman 1996, 299), continues to circulate amongst the general public and inspire individuals.

I have discussed elsewhere some of the manners in which such imaginary con-structs, though they may be 'unreal', are socially efficient (Čurda 2022). As a matter of fact, antiquity discourses on Odissi and other dances are linked to moral values. One famous example is the figure of the female temple dancer of antique times rep-resented as "a pure and holy, chaste woman [...][9]" (Bharucha 1995, 45–46[10]), a repre-sentation that is commonly seen in nationalisms, where "feminised images [...] de-fine the *iconography* of the nation, [while] the *practice* of nationalism is reserved for the male" (Silva 2004, 21[11]). Such constructions serve the purposes of specific social groups involved with the dance practices, and contribute to upholding and legit-imizing a specific social order. In addition, dancers actually physically enact these narratives, for example, by including them repeatedly in their choreographies (e.g. Čurda 2013, 2017, 2022), thereby, endowing them with an embodied existence. The presence of such constructs in collective imagination is, therefore, in no way neu-tral, as they are based on social values and contribute to reinforce and re-actualize these.

---

8   These are in no way exhaustive, and I wish to apologize to any contributor to this debate whom, due to the constraints of this writing, I may not have mentioned.

9   I wish to specify that Bharucha is concerned with Bharata Natyam. However, Odissi has adopted this representation as well.

10   Quoted in Čurda, 2013.

11   Ibid.

Presences on internet sites: conventions and individual choices in self-representation

Now one thing that the Internet is useful for is to publicize and disseminate such discursive constructions. Not surprisingly, conventional representations of Odissi dance and its networks are most readily "available all at once" (Noë 2005, 243) on many websites, notably those of Odissi dance schools. A look at some of them permits one to spot typical contents. In fact, it is quite remarkable to what extent such websites reproduce what I will call a ritualistic stereotypy, suggestive of a great amount of agreement between practitioners on what their dance has to be all about.[12] Schools commonly assert on such websites that they are committed to "popularize Odissi and also retain the purity in this classical dance form",[13] to "preserving and popularizing the rich culture of Odissi",[14] and to "holding firm to the values and traditions"[15] of the dance. One can feel that the agenda with which these write-ups align is very prescriptive, as their authors appear to be driven by a preoccupation to conform to a pre-existing mould. The reader learns that the dance is "pure", "rich" and "traditional" – imbued with values evoking the aspiration to a high cultural status. But beyond that, there is a binary logic underlying these terms. One which often serves the purpose of distinguishing what is conformed to from what is not. The sentences above definitely convey a sense of distinction and exquisiteness, and clearly associate this quality with Odissi. The same websites also carry forth representations of the schools as "a premier training institution"[16] or "one of the leading dance institutions",[17] and of individual practitioners as "one of the most celebrated Odissi Solo artists".[18] Through these expressions, their existences seem to be bound within prescribed modes of action that appear to consist of "ritualistically climbing a ladder" (Van Zile 2001, 56) towards a goal that appears evident, shiny and highly desirable. They are presented in their self-representations on the net as if they were the accomplished embodiments of that goal. Consequently, these types of phenomena do not appear so different from the processes described above: imaginary constructs, whether stigmatizing or enhancing, raise expectations in people's minds. The reader is prompted to react in sensory and emotional manners in accordance with the values they evoke.

---

12   While my inquiry concentrates on practitioners in India – and for the present discussion, in Bhubaneswar – many Odissi dance schools situated elsewhere in the world – even in the US – actually carry along the same type of discursive content.

13   https://www.pragnyanrutyayan.com

14   https://www.srjan.com/

15   https://www.rudrakshyafoundation.org/

16   https://www.srjan.com/

17   https://www.rudrakshyafoundation.org/

18   https://www.pragnyanrutyayan.com

This self-proclaimed magnificence evidently aims at convincing the audience that is potentially virtually present on the net. However, virtual presences could also be quite misleading if our aim is to assess factual phenomena. What could be the concrete situations lying behind such affirmations? Is the goal achieved or achievable? Does it constitute the central theme of ongoing existential struggles? Who are the embodied counterparts to these disembodied presences? But also, one may wish to wonder, who, beyond this selection of individuals who have the power to advertise their activity via the Internet, is present in Odissi networks? In other words, what is the gap between these virtual presences and physical existences? In order to explore this point, I propose to have a look at embodied presences.

Assessing factual presences of practitioners

One of the most common problems the social scientist continually strives to solve is to find ways to generate evidence on things 'as they are'. This, in some way, is not unlike the problem that Noë analyses regarding the tomato. The problem I faced in the particular case of the state of advancement of my research project in September 2021 may be formulated as: How to obtain evidence on the existence of dance activity that does not exclude, in arbitrary ways, some particular groups of participants – or, we may say, specific 'slices of the tomato'? This question is much wider than the divide into embodied and/or disembodied presences allows us to take into consideration.

As I had participated in the networks of Odissi dance as a practitioner in Bhubaneswar since the 1990s, I had ample knowledge on their prior modes of functioning (call for footnote [19]). But I had been out of touch since 2009 and needed to assess recent developments. Since then, the city of Bhubaneswar has continued the explosive expansion that had been initiated ever since this originally insignificant temple town had been declared the capital of the state in 1948.[20] By the onset of the COVID-19 pandemic, it had turned from what had in the 1990s been a rather laidback city into a much busier one, one which, in addition, had been transformed through India's relatively recent impressive economic growth.[21] In parallel, the technological revolution the country had known brought new ways of experiencing social relations. As such rapid developments must have had an impact on the dance networks, it seemed obvious that an investigation promised to uncover many new

---

19 Čurda, 2013.
20 For a comprehensive account of the transformation of Bhubaneswar into a capital city, see Kalia (1994).
21 As a consequence of being nominated as a state capital, the population of Bhubaneswar evolved from 16 512 according to the census of 1951 to 837,737 according to the census figures of 2011 (the latest census figures are estimated to 1,161,000 in 2023: https://www.census20 11.co.in/census/city/270-bhubaneswar.html).

facts. Therefore, my first task was to find out what the activity in this dance field had turned into by 2020. This implies that I focused on existence, considering that some presences may very much escape common perceptions. And it also means that, at this stage of my research, I tended to exclude presences that were part of common perceptions but did not exist.

There are many discriminative factors in social life that render some individuals more noticeable than others. This is of particular importance in relation to a dance practice such as Odissi, in which practitioners spend a lot of energy trying to get into the field of perception of different audiences, for example, art lovers, cultural institutions and journalists. The evocation of the contents of websites above is also a result of individuals' efforts to show their 'best' side to a public, expose their conformity to a set of codes. Not all of them resort to the same means nor do they enjoy the same success rates in obtaining an efficient acknowledgement of their being present as contributors to the Odissi dance field.[22] Their efforts towards obtaining symbolic rewards are even, quite often, linked to a politics of exclusion. The presences of certain people – or of certain types of people – tend not to be taken notice of, while others are perceived more readily. Again, these discriminative practices are actually of scientific interest, and I advocate that it is necessary to examine not only why, but also how certain 'slices of the tomato' rise into higher prominence than others. Accordingly, looking at the prominent 'sides of the tomato' is good scientific practice – provided one takes into account both the less visible and invisible slices. However, I aimed at assessing factual presences in my inquiry, at looking at phenomena that existed – and for this, it was necessary that I did not let myself be influenced by those who might have had more power than others in the dance's networks.

Thus, in my quest for uncovering scientific truth during my recent ethnography in Bhubaneswar from September 2021 onwards, I searched for ways to circumvent the difficulty posed by the fact that many sources of information on practices of a dance form such as Odissi were most likely to be selective. Government bodies dedicated to cultural activity, for example, would provide information based on the level of recognition of individual practitioners. Though this was definitely of interest, it was also insufficient. I also refrained from searching through my own, previously well-known networks in this first stage of my research, as it appeared important to challenge and verify the accuracy of the knowledge of Odissi dance networks I had acquired previously. I did not resort to registering websites, as it was evident that those who could create and maintain a website were, either on their own or through the help of their network, proficient in English, and had either direct or indirect

---

22   Of course, computer literacy and access to computer equipment are not distributed equally within societies, more so in countries like India where inequalities between social groups are particularly prominent. There are many other social criteria, however, that come into consideration regarding such a question.

access to technology and the resources the maintenance of a website requires, all of which are certain types of privileges they enjoyed over others. Of course, no tool existed that would allow one to gain a view of the phenomenon as a whole, as any potential source of information could only provide a view of 'selected slices of the tomato'. Some methods, however, were more likely to hide from me what could potentially be quite interesting facts on dance practitioners' existences.

In order to characterize more accurately the phenomenon of Odissi dance practices in Bhubaneswar in the early 2000s and widen the scope for reaching out to practitioners belonging to a greater variety of social groups, I resorted, for this stage of my research, to a combination of a search on Google Maps, followed by physical visits to addresses identified, as complementary tools for assessing Odissi dance activity in the city. Google Maps appeared interesting because the web mapping platform is not controlled by the practitioners' networks. Therefore, it seemed to be, potentially, relatively insensitive to some discriminative patterns used by Odissi practitioners amongst themselves. Certainly, it could not give an all-encompassing picture of Odissi dance activity, but the criteria by which it registers presences promised to be more inclusive than others.

I fed the search engine with the words "Odissi" and "Bhubaneswar", and the platform returned results of what I broadly circumscribe to be "dance schools". This deserves a bit of elaboration, as I use this expression in the same manner as Odissi practitioners do – and this is, of course, a context-specific use. Without going into the details of the history of the dance and the local concepts of pedagogy,[23] let me mention that practitioners habitually use the term "dance school" each time they relate to a dance class taking place. A part of this happens in places that are officially registered as schools, and another part in places that are not. Amongst registered schools figure not only proper institutional structures but also individual initiatives that deploy their activity in other manners. Thus, a school, in the view of Odissi practitioners, can be a building (i.e. an institution), a private house in which somebody opens up a space to welcome learners, or even a person – because, in some cases, teachers do not have the means to provide a specific space for their dance classes, and may be teaching in diverse locations by soliciting their networks to temporarily provide rooms for practicing dance in all kinds of places. Google Maps, by the entries

---

23   The vernacular concept of *guru-śiṣya-paramparā* (tradition of masters and disciples) is based on the idea of a one-to-one relationship. Even though the actual practice differs from the theory, this idea is valued by individuals.

it indicated as a reply to my search, appeared, to a good extent, to follow the lines of such a conception.[24]

Interestingly, the somewhat hazy typology that resulted from this search excluded a couple of government bodies belonging to the higher education infrastructure of the city, which deliver diplomas that are recognized by the higher education system. However, the results broadly corresponded to what I have above circumscribed with the term "Odissi dance schools", and this context-specific idea of a school appeared appealing in relation to my scientific endeavour. Notably, it comprised the promise to spot, with each new finding, a cluster of people, including dance teachers, dancers and learners. A first survey made me register more than 35 addresses. Given the amount of data produced in this manner, the results were, despite its imperfections, representative. Out of those, as I followed up with physical visits to the locations that had been identified, about 25 were actually found.

In the physical world

While the websites I referred to earlier had led to the identification of discursive constructions, the search in the material world confronted me with a rich variety of corporeal sensations. These frequently seemed strangely withdrawn from the impressions the writings inspected above generate. Many of these sensory experiences were not the ones I would have spontaneously associated with the idea of a high cultural status.

Sensory disturbances

The first spectacular effect the physical activity of making myself present in different places in Bhubaneswar had on me was to update my physical experience of the city, thereby informing me of the impact my embodied presence in the field had on me. I turned into being the observer of how the spectacular changes the city had undergone within about twelve years of my absence affected me, both physically and emotionally. In many ways, this town did not seem to be the one I had known even a decade before. It appeared to me to be alien in various ways, and now, this experience, with all its impressions, became the lens through which I was to perceive Odissi practitioners' existences.

---

24   It would, of course, require an in-depth analysis to demonstrate whether, and also how, the artificial intelligence reproduces people's intentions or conceptions. It may be sufficient here to accept that the patterns of the results matched common conceptions of dance schools sufficiently well.

I could easily cover Bhubaneswar by bicycle during the 1990s and even in the first decade of the 2000s. This would have been absolutely impossible in 2021. To go to particular places, I now frequently had to cover distances that could amount to fifteen kilometres, reach out, in the hot, damp climate, to locations that, in my previous encounters with the city, had been situated beyond its outermost margins. I had to suffer the sensory disturbances generated by the density of the traffic on the streets, which has evolved impressively since I had left. Narrow roads had been replaced by imposing, busy highways in some parts of the city, making me wonder how I could have ever cycled there. The localities that were closer to the city centre looked much neater than in the past. An effort by the Bhubaneswar municipality to make the city look agreeable was visible in many details: the pavements, which had previously been in a miserable condition, presenting holes and fissures, had been upgraded, partly decorated on the outer borders with paint, flower pots and ornamental lanterns. Outer walls visible from the street had been covered with paintings, presenting many different motives (photo 1).

Photo 1: Bhubaneswar 12 February 2022 © Suko Lam

When one reached the outskirts of the city, however, things were quite different: many roads in the new housing colonies were unpaved and uneven. On rainy days, they were often flooded. Some of the individual houses in these parts of the city looked rather neat, others miserable. In both cases, they were surrounded by plots of unbuilt land, paddy fields and, sometimes, the temporary shelters hurriedly put up by workers working on local construction sites. There was frequently a lot of construction work going on in these areas, adding to an overall precarious look. Thus, the first effect of my inquiry was that it shook up my preconceptions of the city, based on my prior experiences. This clearly potentiated the scope of the research. And it is the encounter of my entire body with the material conditions in which inhabitants of Bhubaneswar evolve that enabled this process to take place. Let me, therefore, describe some of it.

Entanglements and disruptions between virtual and physical spaces

Some things require physical experiences to be known. They are beyond imagination. A wild, uncontrollable city growth has plenty of curious effects on the environment. As I was heading towards many different locations in my aim to physically encounter the places I had spotted in the virtual space of Google Maps, I quickly found out that this presented difficulties. One of the most trivial amongst these was that often no one knew how to find a particular address. Conditioned by western modes of locating places in an urban area, I had first searched for a map of Bhubaneswar. I rapidly realized that I could not find any map in the local book stores comprising the details of the localities and of their streets. The owner of a popular book shop presented me with a couple of imprecise maps of the city, simultaneously claiming that nothing better existed on the market, and asserted that no editor had produced any city map that would be conform to what in western Europe would have been common expectations.[25] Furthermore, as I undertook my visits using a local taxi service, I realized that most of the drivers did not have much knowledge of the local topography. Moreover, they were a bit unsettled by my somewhat unconventional demands. It was noticeable that they were not used to having to find a series of addresses in the city. Some of them adapted rather well, and some resorted to the voice direction services on their phones to head out towards the places I was asking them to find. Once again, I was dependent on a virtual tool, but this time in my search for embodied presences. The phone generally turned out to be of uttermost importance as a regulator of not only the drivers' but also other people's sense of geographical space. In instances in which I had difficulties in finding a place, for example, individuals I would ask for directions would advise me to call the people I was to meet on the phone.

I quickly found myself confronted with unexpected peculiarities that the margins of the city presented. I found it particularly difficult, for example, to reach certain places when, arriving in a locality after having made many rounds with my driver, I had to face the fact that all the houses of the street I was heading to share the same plot number. Which one, then, could be the house I was looking for? Another variation of this consequence of the rapid rate of construction was a chaotic

---

25   Reading geographical maps does not appear to have been a common or valued practice among the local populations in different parts of India. I thank Kannan Muthukrishnan for pointing this out with reference to the State of Tamil Nadu.

distribution of plot numbers: sometimes, finding a house would turn out to be particularly difficult, because numbers in a lane did not follow each other in numerical order, so that one could not spot a house by logical deduction.

Another point that turned the visits of the outskirts of the city into a sensory challenge were gaps between the physical and the virtual world of Google Maps. It seemed that space could not be explored easily. In a few instances, the mismatch between the virtual topography and the concrete environment forced me to modify my itinerary. In one situation, for example, after having inspected several lane in a part of the city, I found myself unable to locate the house number for which I was searching. After having toured the place for a while, I finally realized that a small bridge that had crossed a stream was broken, so that the lane ended abruptly. The bridge still existed on Google Maps, and this is why the voice direction application that my driver had used had lead us to the particular spot in which we had landed. The house for which I was searching was actually on the other side of the broken bridge, and it was impossible to get there from where I was situated.

Even more mysterious was my encounter with another street when I returned to a location after a gap of about two months. The main street of a new residential area, situated at one edge of the city, was fully blocked. Some construction work was occurring on a section of it (photo 2). That part was completely covered with some vegetation that had been disposed there, lying on the ground, as if it was to be planted. It was quite a strange sight: the way to the location I was heading to was obstructed, and the street seemed to be transformed into something other than a street, and yet, it was the main thoroughfare providing access to this particular locality.

Photo 2: Bhubaneswar 25 December 2021 © Suko Lam

Such peculiarities could appear and disappear with great rapidity in relatively short time spans. In the case of the broken bridge, when I returned to the same place a couple of months later, a new bridge had already been built there. Construction work was still going on, and the surroundings looked unruly, as there were piles of sand all over the place. The virtual mapping system and the physical world were, however, coherent again.

These situations made me associate the experience of the outskirts of the city with a strong sense of uncertainty. Yet, what counts here is that the wild growth of Bhubaneswar constitutes the spatio-temporal context in which the lives of Odissi practitioners unfold. Wherever in town they are situated, and whatever their socio-economic backgrounds may be, their lives, and their lives as dancers acting within and reacting to the environment in which their dance practices develop, be it in their corporeal or economic dimensions, are imbricated with the dynamics of the urban development.

Socially situated spaces

Material spaces provide hints to many factors that shape the lives of individuals, including the socio-economic conditions they may be experiencing, their gender and cultural backgrounds. In some cases, the materiality is in itself sufficient to come to certain conclusions, while in others, it requires a reading of this materiality, an interpretation based on knowledge about its social significance in the local context. I give some examples here to illustrate this – notably, the question of the distribution of Odissi practitioners in the urban spaces, the relation between material spaces and gender, and the question of what was at stake when presences turned out to be difficult to spot.

Patterns of Odissi dancers' presence in town

City margins are often, in many places, commonly associated with lower income groups. But this does not always hold true, and in the quickly growing city of Bhubaneswar, even the outskirts provide shelter to a great variety of social groups, both underprivileged and advantaged. However, similar to elsewhere, some of the physical characteristics of the residences in which people live hint at their belonging to particular classes. One physical evidence of the impact of urbanization is the distribution of the dance schools within the topography of the city: Odissi practitioners are actually found to be present anywhere in Bhubaneswar, from the city centre to the outermost limits of the newly urbanized areas, where paddy fields coexist with new constructions of either individual or collective housing. These spatial elements give some type of feedback on their existences and the constraints in which they evolve. The choice to shift to newly urbanized areas indicates a good degree of mobility. Thus, those dance practitioners who seize the opportunities of such rapid city developments evolve in inconstant settlement conditions. Additionally, one of the most common motives to move to the outer margins of the city is to avail themselves of comparatively better living conditions at a better price. Another point is that several indications such as this one, added together, contribute to providing insight, step by step, into emotional, economic and relational aspects of the existences of Odissi practitioners.

Gendered presences

In some cases, insider knowledge is needed to decode certain social characteristics. When identifying dance schools, for example, I associated those that were located within collective housing buildings with femininity. As a matter of fact, each time my search unearthed a collective housing building, the person behind that particular school turned out to be a woman (photo 3). Again, when I spotted a school in a somewhat desolate looking area, located in a precarious looking construction consisting of one floor, with an asbestos roof, my presumption that the person leading it was male turned out to be correct (photo 4). This is due to the combined facts that multistorey buildings, a relatively recent addition to the architecture of Bhubaneswar, are locally considered as more classy than individual housing.[26] In addition, Odissi's development, from its onset from the 1950s onwards, has been based on a sharp social divide between male practitioners from relatively low income groups, who recently migrated to the city, and female practitioners belonging to diverse strata of an earlier urbanized population (for a detailed account see Čurda 2013, 67–122). Consequently, the women practicing the dance, on average, still belong to higher status groups than the men. Male and female practitioners are, therefore, present in spaces that convey very different sensations, and these have strong connotations regarding their social status.

---

26   The facades of such buildings did not always match that idea: in one case, one building presented a facade that had been fully washed out by the monsoon rains; in another, I entered a spooky staircase which I would in no way have associated with higher living standards, before entering a rather elegant looking flat; and in two cases, these buildings were situated in the very far outskirts, surrounded by rice fields and greenery, where I would not have suspected to be able to find comfortable middle- to upper-class housing.

Photo 3: Bhubaneswar 14 February 2022 © Suko Lam

Photo 4: Bhubaneswar 14 February 2022 © Suko Lam

Discreet presences

I here turn my attention to what, following Noë's logic, are the "hidden sides of the tomato". Some presences turned out to be discreet, others were even elusive. Yet, knowing about them made a difference to my assessment. In many ways, a good number of Odissi dance schools I looked up did not leave any prominent imprint of their presences on the environment. This, again, is an indicator of the actual conditions within which the dancers organize their activity. This particularity contrasts sharply with the discourses found on Odissi dance schools' websites, which were so suggestive of a high level of recognition for the dance and individual practitioners.

A lot of schools had no signboards. Nothing indicated their presence in the streets in which I searched for them. Later, in the course of my research, some dance teachers told me that because they were teaching in their homes, which they occupied on a rented basis, their landlords objected to their putting up a signboard in the street. Not having the means to unfold one's activity within what would be a 'professional' environment suggests that the practices evolve, amongst others, via non-formalized relationships. This has many reasons. One of them is that historically, relations between practitioners are not necessarily tied to formalized institutional structures. It is socially perfectly acceptable that even a teacher who has a good reputation may give private classes rather than be tied up within institutional structures. But the landlords' attitudes are relevant too: there is a stark contrast between the fact that Odissi is represented to constitute national heritage, and that the people practicing this dance do not seem to have the authority to get their activities advertised and officialized. Additionally, I was amazed by the low level of response when frequently I asked people on the road for directions while searching for a school. Many individuals on the streets did not know about the dance schools – even schools which, from the point of view of Odissi practitioners, were the most prominent. It seemed that dance practices were not of concern to the general public.

Some schools were also discreet in other ways: In some situations, the address indicated for a school was not the address of the location where the dance activity took place but that of the domicile where the teacher lived. In such cases, the actual teaching activity often took place in several parts of the city. Certain practitioners do not have the means to rent a space for teaching dance. It is not uncommon that they commute to different locations in the city. Some of them partly impart their teaching in the form of individual classes, and even when they teach a group of people, it takes place in all sorts of locations that are temporarily made available either on a rented basis or without financial counterpart, at the initiative of diverse well-wishers. I could confirm in the subsequent phase of my research that, in specific cases, this type of unsettled teaching activity was an indicator of a rather low socio-economic status. Among the situations I encountered, there was a person who used to commute to several places in town to get her work done. Her rehearsals for a show took place in a centrally located ashram – it turned out that she had a privileged relationship with its religious leader – and she was giving some of her dance classes in a school for disabled people in a part of the town situated far away from the ashram. In the school, a room was temporarily transformed, a few evenings a week, into a hall for dancing. This particular type of activity was most circumscribed when I started my research in September, and only picked up when the sanitary situation slowly relaxed. So, many presences were unstable, not connected to a constant place in space,

distributed over several areas of the town – which constitutes a kind of precariousness.

Elusive presences

It was easy to make out that the pandemic had a strong impact on Odissi dance
teaching in the city. In quite a few cases, I ventured upon people whose schools were
temporarily closed. The interior of one government institution I visited appeared
ghost-like to me, as only a few administrative staff members were present in its otherwise empty, huge spaces. In other situations, some of the people I met told me that
they had resorted to teaching in virtual ways, mostly by using apps, such as WhatsApp. Most of them told me that they were not very enthusiastic about this way of
teaching, yet it helped them overcome the material aspects of the crisis.

In some instances, when I found an address, I was told that the school had existed, but had moved. In one such case, the physical encounter allowed me to discover an economic fact, as I learnt that the reason why one school had disappeared
was the economic distress the pandemic had caused for its teacher.

In some cases, I did not find the school I searched for at the address indicated,
yet the result of the investigation was informative. In one situation, for example, I
met a family at an address indicated in Google Maps. They showed great surprise on
hearing that a dance school appeared to exist at their home address on the virtual
map. However, they guessed that a male dance teacher who had been giving private
classes to their daughter in their home might have used their address in order to
register a school. The presence of this school on Google Maps was a consequence of
the fact that this person did not have the means to register an address of his own. In
this case, instead of finding a school, I found out about a network of interconnected
individuals and learnt about its way of functioning.

In some cases, my search did not return any result at all. Many times, I toured
all the lanes in a housing colony, searching repeatedly for a place without any success. I would generally ask a few people in the street whether they knew about any
dance school. Sometimes, even though a school was difficult to find, some people
appeared to have some awareness of the existence of something of that sort. However, very frequently, they would not know anything. This added further to an overall
impression of inconstancy.

Bridging the gap between virtual and physical presences

Discreet and elusive presences, as well as absences, constitute data and contribute,
alone or in relation to virtual findings, to a process of interrogating continuities and
discontinuities of individual activities, generating an understanding of the state of
Odissi dance networks in Bhubaneswar in the 2020s. My research methodology then

was part of a process "of gathering or assembling content" (Noë 2005, 249), witnessing the sensory aspects of the everyday lives of those who teach Odissi dance. These were loaded with indices about the environmental conditions in which people live, with their distinctive roughness, indications about the social backgrounds to which they belong and about the impact of the sanitary crisis on their dance activities. The sensory experience of encountering locations, the roughness associated to their physicality, disconnected me from the idea of magnificence that is found in common representations of the dance. Virtual presences of Odissi practitioners on the net seemed to be a mismatch with the surroundings of the city.

Yet, it is in one of my informal meetings with a male dance teacher at his home, a small, insignificant looking individual house with a little garden, situated in a commercial area of Bhubaneswar just across from a slum, that the discourses on recognition within the networks of Odissi practitioners and by the local cultural institutions reappeared with force in relation to himself. Looking at this man in conversation within the surroundings of his small living room overloaded with furniture, the words he pronounced in order to situate himself as one of the established teachers of the dance appeared to me in another light. In the situation of our face-to-face presence, the contrast between what he said, and how and where it was said, indicated to me his struggle to maintain a position in Odissi's circles. This underlined the importance symbolic rewards could have for him in the context of the hardships of material life.

It is then important to consider that both these phenomena – the harshness of the physical world and the smooth representation existences of Odissi practitioners find in the virtual one – are not necessarily exclusive of each other. These findings are, instead, reminiscent of a more analytical view on artists in societies in the West, where, as Zukin suggests, the mass media circulate "images of cool" (1995, 9) about artistic practices, which are "divorced from their social context" (Ibid.). In reference to New York, Zukin states that "'high' cultural producers are supposed to live on the margins; and the incomes of most visual artists, art curators, actors, writers, and musicians suggest they must be used to deprivation" (Ibid., 13). Are artistic trajectories in Bhubaneswar, the places of artists in society, comparable to that? It would be premature to jump to conclusions, given the great differences in the cultural backgrounds of the two locations. Moreover, the data provided here on the existences of Odissi practitioners would deserve to be completed by more detailed information on their economic situations. Yet the idea that culture serves the purpose, for those who engage with it intensely, to transcend the hardships of their lives, as they view "their 'real' identity" (Ibid., 13) as connected to their artistic practice, is seen in both societies. In the Oriya, and even the broader Indian context, it is encapsulated in a vernacular conception according to which an artist has to dedicate his or her full life to the artistic practice – an idea that is not void of a sacrificial dimension.

Though "culture is a system for producing symbols" (Ibid., 12), the contrast between the precarious aspects of the immediate environment and a glimmering imaginary life are not limited to artistic practices. In many ways, the visual dimension of urban life in Bhubaneswar carries forth this contradiction. A common example is that of publicity slogans, such as the phrase "this 2022 Bhubaneswar will dawn a new era of high living" on an advertising poster at the foot of which lies some minor waste, raised in the middle of a dusty street lined with desolate-looking walls, in the middle of busy traffic (photo 5). The slogan seems to promise relief from the too evident weight of unkempt surroundings, left to gradual decay by the municipality. This type of sight is perfectly characteristic of the outer aspects of Indian cities, a point which underlines the importance of utopias of prosperity in people's emotional lives.

Photo 5: Bhubaneswar 29 December 2021 © Suko Lam

I would like to get back to the sentence by Layton quoted earlier in this article: "our mind becomes manifest in the objects, traces, and leavings that we generate during our lifetime" (2003, 458). This statement is based on Gell's concept of "distributed personhood" (1998), which leans on the idea that artefacts bring forth the intentions of their creators, as the object created has significance in relation to the position of its creator in a relational network. In fact, the lines above make me wonder: Is it the Odissi dancers' minds that become manifest in the conventional write-ups on their practices?

This relates to the question of agency. In the sense brought forth by Giddens (1984), agency refers to people's – but in our case also non-human's – capacity to act. From the point of view of Gell, agency is relational, and involves not only an agent but also a patient (1998). This implies that in a relationship between "persons, things, animals, divinities, in fact, anything at all" (Ibid., 22), someone or something, at different points of time, is temporarily either an agent or a patient – the actant or the one who is being acted upon.

The presences encountered during my inquiry in the physical world show how the living conditions in a particular place exert their agency on individuals who, in relation to these, become patients. Things, by their presence, act on people, constricting them at times, modifying their ways of being in the world. Individuals are bound to react, immediately, to their concrete situations. And this overall context speaks about them being male, female, forced to respond to economic imperatives, at times able and at other times unable to make a difference. What is sure is that their being dancers cannot be thought without their being people experiencing the impact of their environment – physical and social – on them.[27] Yet, the dreamlike exposition of the dances' exquisiteness may still be part of their ways of experiencing the world. The teacher mentioned above utilized it in his discursive exposition of his achievements in order to reclaim agency over his existence, even while he occupied the position of a patient regarding his immediate living conditions. This situation, in which imaginary constructions place an individual into the agent's position, can, of course, not be generalized – as the same discursive patterns may also be used in order to make a person occupy the place of a patient. However, in all these examples so far, it is the physical person's presence which defines their state as an agent or a patient. Does not the idea of distributed presence – the presence of a person in something else than the person herself, bring to this discussion dimensions that are much more complex? I would like to illustrate this with an example.

This anecdote dates back to May 2022. I am sitting in my office at my research institute in India. The room is comfortably big. All the walls are covered with shelves containing innumerable library books. I am surrounded by five colleagues who, like me, work silently throughout the day, as if they were tied to the spaces of their specific desks. In this place, we hardly talk or make any sound which could potentially disrupt the others' activities. An untold rule seems to exist that makes us avoid engaging in any activity that generates noise. I sometimes get so engrossed in my tasks that I become unaware of my colleagues.

---

27   Julien and Rosselin (2003), in their discussion on the production of French Chinese lacquered furniture in Paris, argue that the production of a technical object can in no way be separated from whatever objects or circumstances – be they historic, geographical, spatial, social – impacted its final shape. This furniture's production, for example, started thriving when, in the 1930s, Chinese students who had no prior experience in the production of furniture took up small jobs in order to finance their studies, and provided an air of authenticity for the furniture by their embodied presence. The examples brought up in relation to Odissi practitioners reveal the same type of connectedness between, for example, human beings, objects and socio-economic situations.

Sometimes, during this period, I receive an e-mail from a colleague in France: the person says that I am connected to a seminar session in my home university in France, and is demanding that we have a videoconference. She seems discontent with not having been able to videoconference with me. I am, in fact, unaware of being connected to any virtual meeting. It is only through the e-mail that I am made aware of the fact that something she considers to be me is present eight thousand kilometres away, in this very moment. I suppose the connection to be real, however, I have not activated it knowingly. The experience of my presence by my colleague in a virtual seminar further contradicts my own experience of my physical presence, in a room where my body is surrounded by other bodies, and obeys the corporeal order imposed by their presences – and this order does not allow me to engage in activities that generate sound, such as videoconferencing.

The distribution of my presence constitutes, in fact, a multiplication of it. Moreover, that which is multiplied has, in my perception, nothing at all to do with me. In fact, while my colleague may be in a position to say that my presence exerts agency on her – I am feeling overwhelmed by what presence in the twenty-first century does to me. The impact of virtuality on my life that I experience through this episode seems to have robbed me of my agency. This example seems to talk about my distributed presence – distributed simultaneously in two locations situated about eight thousand kilometers from each other. But it is also about me manifesting a certain distress about being represented to be present somewhere in a way that contradicts my perception. From my subjective point of view, it questions how true the allegation of me being present eight thousand kilometers away might be. It has some characteristic that make it resemble hallucinatory presences. This example highlights how powerful perceived presence can be. And it puts up questions that are highly relevant for our existence, which revolve around not only the sense that we may find in the different ways in which we are made present to others, but also, the question of the factual existences of what is being perceived.

Conclusion

My underlying line of thought throughout these pages was the question of what presences do to us, how what they do to us differs according to the type of presence and how this affects what we are able to know. In relation to this, I have been mentioning the suggestive dimension of virtual or imagined presences of Odissi practitioners, and the way these underline the magnificent aspects of their activity. I have been demonstrating how their physical presences, be it just in visual ways, contradict such assertions. The encounters with school buildings, with the people who are leading those schools, and with the town areas in which they are evolving, constituted confrontations with a physical environment, generating sensory experiences. So, the presences of people became manifest not only through their own bodies, but also through the materialities that constituted their living environment. These added density to the experiences of listening to people's words, and inferred their interpretation. Encountering embodied presences was a process which made apparent individuals' embeddedness in social, urban, relational and environmental contexts by physically encountering the networks of living and non-living beings that were part of their daily experiences of life. It made them appear more trivial, less in command of their destinies, a particularity which made me react in a much more empathetic manner.

Examining these presences led me to note to which extent virtual and physical presences may, at times, be entangled – this is prominent, for example, when individuals use phones to find a place. In such circumstances, virtuality has by now modified the cognitive modalities they use in order to orient themselves in space. In other situations, virtuality and physicality appear less dependent on each other. They may even be in opposition – this is the case, for example, when a person asserted that I was present in a place in which I was not; in another manner, the imaginary constructions about Odissi appeared to be in contradiction with the physical conditions in which practitioners live. What seems to separate virtual encounters from physical ones is the density of sensory experiences involved in both ways of meeting. Whether presences are virtual or physical, the examples have shown that perceived presence – or the subjective experience of presence – has, to extents that vary from one case to another, its degree of social efficiency. However, and this may be a central point of these lines, different ways of being present – virtually or physically, in human, non-human, alive or inert ways – contribute to a different reading of social life, and are, therefore, highly relevant to people's lives.

Bibliography

Bharucha, Rustom. 1995. Chandralekha. Woman Dance Resistance. New Delhi: HarperCollins Publishers India Pvt Ltd.

Carli, Dafne. 2000. Les enfants du seigneur de sable – Aux racines de la danse odissi. DESS d'Ethnologie. Université Denis Diderot – Paris VII.

Čurda, Barbara. 2013. Enjeux identitaires, relationnels et esthétiques de la transmission de la danse Odissi en Inde – Le cas d'une école émergente à Bhubaneswar dans l'Etat d'Orissa [Identity, Relational and Aesthetic Issues in the Transmission of Odissi Dance in India. The Case of an Emerging Dance School in Bhubaneswar in the State of Orissa]. Doctoral Dissertation, Clermont-Ferrand: Université Blaise Pascal de Clermont-Ferrand.

Čurda, Barbara. 2017. "Establishing Lineages through Discursive and Choreographic Practices: Odissi Dancers' References to Mahari and Gotipua Dances."

Dance, Senses, Urban Contexts. 29th Symposium of the ICTM Study Group on Ethnochoreology, edited by Kendra Stepputat, 92–6. Herzogenrath: Shaker Verlag.

Čurda, Barbara. 2022. "Le «réel», le «virtuel», et les mythes d'antiquité des danses «classiques indiennes» : le cas de la danse Odissi." Pratiques artistiques et culturelles : jeux du réel et du virtuel entre plausible et incroyable [en ligne], edited by Véronique Dassié. Paris: Éditions du Comité des travaux historiques et scientifiques. http://books.openedition.org/cths/16311.

Durkheim, Emile. 1895. Les règles de la méthode sociologique. Paris: Félix Alcan.

Erdman, Joan L. 1996. "Dance Discourses: Rethinking the History of the 'Oriental Dance'." Moving Words: Re-writing Dance, edited by Gay Morris. London, New York: Routledge.

Fratagnoli, Federica. 2010. Les danses savantes de l'Inde à l'épreuve de l'Occident: formes hybrides et contemporaines du religieux. Doctoral thesis, Université Paris 8.

Gaston, Anne-Marie. 1996. Bharata Natyam – From Temple to Theatre. New Delhi: Manohar.

Gell, Alfred. 1998. Art and Agency: An Anthropological Theory. Oxford, New York: Clarendon Press.

Giddens, Anthony. 1984. The Constitution of Society: Outline of the Theory of Structuration. Cambridge: Polity Press.

Hobsbawm, Eric, and Terence Ranger (Eds). 1983. The Invention of Tradition. Cambridge: Cambridge University Press.

Julien, Marie-Pierre, and Céline Rosselin. 2003. "C'est en laquant qu'on devient laqueur. De l'efficacité du geste à l'action sur soi." Techniques & Culture 40 (avril 2003). https://doi.org/10.4000/tc.1454.

Kalia, Ravi. 1994. Bhubaneswar: From a Temple Town to a Capital City. Carbondale, IL: Southern Illinois University Press.

Layton, Robert. 2003. "Art and Agency: A Reassessment." Journal of the Royal Anthropological Institute 9(3) 2003: 447–64. https://doi.org/10.1111/1467-9655.0015 8.

Leucci, Tiziana. 2008. "L'apprentissage de la danse en Inde du sud et ses transformations au XXe siècle: le cas des devadasi, rajadasi et nattuvanar." Rivista di studi sudasiatici III: 49–83. Universita degli studi Firenze, Firenze. 2008.

Lopez Y Royo, Alessandra. 2007. "The Reinvention of Odissi Classical Dance as a Temple Ritual." The Archaeology of Ritual, edited by Evangelos Kyriakidis, 155–82. Los Angeles, CA: Cotsen Institute of Archaeology, University of California.

Malinowsky, Bronislaw. 1922. Argonauts of the Western Pacific. London: Routledge.

Merton, Robert K. 1948. "The Self-Fulfilling Prophecy." The Antioch Review 8(2): 193. https://doi.org/10.2307/4609267.

Noë, Alva. 2005. "Real Presence." Philosophical Topics 33(1): 235–64. https://doi.org/
10.5840/philtopics20053319 .

Noë, Alva. 2006. "Experience of the World in Time." Analysis 66(1): 26–32. https://w
ww.jstor.org/stable/25597696.

Pouchepadass, Jacques. 2000. "Les Subaltern Studies ou la critique postcoloniale de
la modernité." L'Homme 156: 161–86.

Reed, Susan Anita. 2010. Dance and the Nation: Performance, Ritual, and Politics
in Sri Lanka. Studies in Dance History. Madison, WI: University of Wisconsin
Press.

Rodier, Géraldine. 2004. La danse Odissi: un miroir de femmes – Evolution des va-
leurs et représentations de la féminité dans la danse Odissi. DEA d'anthropolo-
gie, Université de Provence, Aix-Marseille 1.

Said, Edward W., 1978. Orientalism – Western Conceptions of the Orient. New
Delhi: Penguin Books India.

Shah, Purnima. 2002. "State Patronage in India: Appropriation of the 'Regional' and
'National'." Dance Chronicle 25(1): 125–41. https://doi.org/10.1081/DNC-1200031
23.

Schnepel, Cornelia. 2005. Odissi – Eine ostindische Tanzform im Kontext der
Debatten um regionale Traditionen und kulturelle Identität, Südasienwissen-
schaftliche Arbeitsblätter. Band 6. Halle: Institut für Indologie und Südasien-
wissenschaften der Martin-Luther-Universität Halle-Wittenberg.

Silva, Neluka. 2004. The Gendered Nation: Contemporary Writings from South Asia.
New Delhi, Thousand Oaks, London: Sage.

Soneji, Davesh. 2012. Unfinished Gestures – Devadasis, Memory, and Modernity in
South India. Chicago: University of Chicago Press.

Subramanian, Lakshmi. 2006 [2011]. From the Tanjore Court to the Madras Music Academy. A Social History of Music in South India, Oxford, New York, New
Delhi: Oxford University Press.

Van Zile, Judy. 2001. Perspectives on Korean dance. Middletown, CO: Wesleyan University Press.

Zukin, Sharon. 1995. The Cultures of Cities. Malden, MA, Oxford, UK: Blackwell Publishers.

Forced and Uncertain Co-presence. Smart Cameras and Distant Homework Supervision in Eastern China

Zhenwei Wang

Abstract *In this chapter, an argument about a new modality of information and communications technology-based co-presence termed 'forced and uncertain co-presence' is developed based on the empirical analysis of the use of smart cameras in distant homework supervision in Eastern China. Drawing on a long-term ethnography of migrant parents installing monitoring cameras on the children's study table and watching them do homework from afar, I observe a close supervision of children's homework and a high level of involvement in their school study among Chinese migrant parents. However, the use of smart cameras deprived the children of the right to control their own presence and brought about what I call 'forced co-presence'. It also produces 'uncertain co-presence', meaning that the state of co-presence is not measured until the parents retrieve the data from the camera as they review the recorded video or read the message transmitted by the artificial intelligence to their phone. The 'forced and uncertain co-presence' has a negative impact on children's emotional experiences with their parents at a distance. They feel controlled, untrusted and insecure under the invisible watch. In conclusion, the practice of smart monitoring enriches the concept of co-presence and sheds light on translocal and transnational family studies in digital times. Although the analysis is based on translocal homework supervision experiences in Eastern China, the concept of 'forced and uncertain co-presence' may be applicable to wider societies as smart monitoring has increasingly been used in child and elderly care since the COVID-19 pandemic.*

Keywords *translocal parenting; migration; copresence; monitoring; China*

Introduction

Home monitoring is especially popular among translocal families in Eastern China. During China's great internal migration, many middle generations migrated to work in the city while the children and elderly stayed behind in the village (Chen, Liu, and Mair 2011; Murphy 2020). At first, monitoring cameras were only installed by migrants at the entrance of their village house for security reasons. Soon, as cameras were combined with a microphone, loudspeaker and cloud storage and equipped with artificial intelligence (AI) that allows them to analyse video in real-time (Chong 2022), migrant parents started to install the cameras above the children's study desk to supervise them doing homework at night. The AI can mark the specific time at which the child appears and leaves the desk and transmit the information to the parents' smartphones. With the livestreaming videos and the text-based AI reports, the migrant parents can create a strong sense of co-presence for the children without sharing the same geographical location or staying with them constantly.

Smart cameras have become affordable and accessible for ordinary Chinese people in recent years. The monitoring industry has grown quickly in China since the state announced its SkyNet Project in 2007 to establish a widely distributed video surveillance network in urban areas and its SnowLight Project in 2015 to extend the surveillance network to rural areas of counties, townships and villages (Li 2017). According to the 2017 documentary *Amazing China*, which was produced by China Central Television and the Publicity Department of the Chinese Communist Party, more than 20 million monitoring cameras have been installed in China. The huge investment in the relevant industry advances the technology and lowers the price of smart monitoring devices. A simple video camera in China can be as cheap as 10 yuan (around 1.3 euros), while an interactive camera with loudspeakers, a connection to a smartphone and real-time AI image processing technology costs about 90 yuan (around 12 euros). The devices are also easily accessible, as they are available both on shopping websites online and at local supermarkets for ordinary customers. Advertisements for smart cameras are widely posted on social media, such as Tik Tok, and they are transmitted to migrants repeatedly according to the recommendation algorithms developed by AI.

In such a context, smart cameras are increasingly used as a communication tool for translocal families in China. Despite their popularity, how smart cameras are transforming the experience of co-presence and how this affects the quality of parent-child relationships at distance is understudied. To fill these gaps, this study examines the experiences of facilitated homework supervision with smart cameras from the perspectives of the migrant parents and the children left behind. Two specific questions are explored: (a) What kind of co-presence is experienced during distant homework supervision via smart cameras, and (b) how does the use of smart cameras affect the quality of parent-child relationships? In this chapter, co-presence is defined as a shared perception of relatedness between the interactants (Alinejad 2019; Montanari and Schlinzig 2022), which is acknowledged to be essential for the production of kinship ties (Carsten 2000). The scholarly discussions on the importance of distant co-presence in translocal family construction is reviewed in the next section.

Constructing distant co-presence, and doing family translocally

Physical proximity used to be vital for enabling co-presence because the temporal and spatial commonality could maximize the abundance of symptoms in human interactions, as argued by Schütz and Luckmann (1974, 66), and because it allowed multidimensional information exchange during social interactions, as argued by Goffman (1983). However, as the development of information and communication technologies (ICTs) has enabled people to connect as if the interactant across a long distance is 'really there', physical proximity and face-to-face interaction are no longer premises of 'doing family' in contemporary digital societies. With the development of new media, spatially dispersed families can communicate and care about each other at high frequency and low expense. They can create stable emotional and social bonds in migration and multilocal living arrangements (Montanari and Schlinzig 2022).

Based on observations of how people sustain family relationships across borders, Baldassar (2008) identified two other forms of co-presence: proxy and virtual. Proxy co-presence is facilitated by special tangible objects, including photos, letters, cards and gifts that embody the spirit of the absent person. These tangible objects function as a substitute for the absence of being, and also represent the incorporeal feelings of love and lack of presence. Virtual copresence, also termed as "ICTs-based co-presence" in Baldassar's other work (2016), is commonly constructed through discursive information exchange via video calls, phone calls, SMS messages or emails. In a later work, she identifies the contrasting modalities of virtual co-presence mediated by various communication tools (Baldassar 2016). Co-presence constructed during video calls on Skype, for example, is immediate, while that produced during text exchange via WhatsApp is more intermediate. However, immediacy has both pros and cons. Video chat can produce a sense of togetherness effectively, but can also result in long and meandering conversations in the end. Texting cannot deliver multisensory information or a sense of togetherness in the moment, but it does give individuals greater autonomy in communication, such as when to read and respond. Hence, Baldassar argues that the new forms of communication do not always replace old forms but rather enrich the polymedia environment that can function as a 'vibrant matter' and facilitate the family to be together across distance.

The notion of a "polymedia environment" was first proposed by Madianou and Miller (2012). They argue that the individual communicative medium is relational in the context of all other media, and it is important to understand how polymedia, as an environment for communication, shapes the experiences of interpersonal relationships. Based on the theory of polymedia, Madianou (2016) identified a new form of co-presence and termed it "ambient co-presence". She observed an increasing prevalence of ubiquitous connectivity enabled by the 'news feed' of social networking sites, which gives rise to a peripheral awareness of distant others without engaging in purposeful or intentional contacting actions. In this kind of co-presence, although awareness of other people's presence is peripheral, the co-presence experience is pervasive and intense. Thus, it can enhance one's sense of belonging to a dispersed family or a community, on the one hand, and create a sense of social surveillance, on the other.

"Ordinary co-presence", another mode of co-presence emerging in the context of polymedia, is proposed by Nedelcu and Wyss (2016). The notion of 'family' over the last twenty years has been more widely understood as an ongoing accomplishment and a result of kinning practices than as a biologically based and spatially bounded social institution in both anthropology and sociology (Strathern 1992; Carsten 2000; Finch 2007; Morgan 2011; Sahlins 2013). Following the practice turn in family and kinship studies, Nedelcu and Wyss (2016) argue that the matrix of ICT-based communications can facilitate family construction across distance by developing online family routines. As long as people construct ritual, omnipresent and reinforced interactions via new media regularly, they can do their families without staying spatially proximate to each other.

These scholarly works challenge the centrality of physical co-presence in family making, and all emphasize the importance of new media technologies in shaping novel ways of doing and practicing families in the contemporary digital world. My research intends to further the ICT-based co-presence studies by focusing on the novice communicative technology of 'smart cameras', which are also called 'interactive home cameras' and 'talking cameras' in everyday life by Chinese people. Monitoring cameras were originally invented for security purposes but are now commonly used for parent-child communication and child supervision in China. Regarding young infants, parents install baby monitors to check their child from another room; for school-aged children, parents use two-way talking cameras to communicate with them and supervise them doing homework. In this chapter, I focus on the distant homework supervision practices between migrant parents and their stay-at-home children and explore how the increasing use of smart monitoring cameras can enrich the concept of co-presence as well as what consequences it may bring to the parent-child relationship in translocal families.

The research and empirical context

This chapter arose out of a larger study concerning translocal kinning and caregiving in Eastern China. The ethnographic fieldwork for the larger study was conducted over ten months between 2020 and 2021 in four locations in Eastern China: the city of Hangzhou where the migrant informants work, Peach Blossom County in northern Zhejiang province, Dragon Village in southern Anhui province and East Town in eastern Jiangxi province, where the migrant informants come from and some of their family members still live[1]. During the fieldwork, I conducted in-depth interviews with 48 people, participant observation of 19 families and informal talks with over 170 people. Not all informants had experience with child monitoring, therefore, this chapter is mainly based on participant observations with three families that installed smart cameras for child supervision, 28 pieces of interview transcripts with in-depth discussions around distant homework supervision, and 15 pieces of discussions on parenting via smart camera on social media of Weibo and Xiaohongshu.

Among the three families that installed smart cameras for child supervision, Family Wen and Family Liu identified themselves as lower-income families, and Family Zheng identified themselves as a middle-income family. The migrant father of Family Wen bought two monitoring cameras for 88 yuan (about 11 euros) and 174 yuan (about 23 euros) in 2020. The cheaper one was installed at the entrance of the house to record the yard and the gate for household security. The more expensive one was installed in the room of the two elementary schoolgirls for homework supervision. The migrant mother of Family Liu bought the monitoring camera for 120 yuan (about 16 euros) in 2018 and installed it on the ceiling of the dining room facing the dining table, on which the family has meals and the elementary school daughter does her homework. The migrant parents of Family Zheng spent 160 yuan (about 21 euros) on two monitoring cameras in 2019. One is installed at the entrance hall and the other in the junior high schoolboy's bedroom, where he studies at night. I visited the homes of all these families in both Hangzhou and the village and observed how they practice distant homework supervision in person.

The 28 interviews were conducted with 14 migrants (8 female and 6 male), 6 stay-at-home elderly people (3 female and 3 male), and 8 stay-at-home teenagers attending junior and senior high school (3 female and 5 male). The interviews last between 40 and 130 minutes, and were all conducted one-to-one in person. I also talked to four elementary schoolchildren and two kindergarten children informally when their adult supervisors were nearby. Because the conversations are unstructured, unrecorded and noted down in the fieldnotes, they are not counted as interviews but as part of the field observation.

The discussions on camera-facilitated parenting on social media were collected from March to September 2021. Ten pieces of discussion were collected from Xiaohongshu, and each has over 40 pieces of comment. Five pieces of discussion (including two videos) were collected from Weibo, and each has over 200 comments. All these discussions were posted by migrant parents. Among the 15 pieces of discussion, 6 are about how they got to know about smart cameras and comparisons of cameras of different brands. Nine pieces are about their experiences of distant homework supervision via camera.

---

1   Peach Blossom County, Dragon Village and East Town are pseudonyms.

The analysis of the data mentioned above is again embedded in the broad project of distant caregiving and family making in China. It cannot be separated from the background knowledge I have learnt during the long-term immersion in the field-work site and the daily interactions with the informants. The conversations about their anxieties regarding a better life, motivation for migration, understandings of their own childhood and relationship with their employers are not directly relevant to the topic of 'distant homework supervision via smart cameras' but provide me with rich material to understand their words between the lines and help me avoid interpreting their practices arrogantly from my own perspective. In this chapter, I want to give the migrant parents and their stay-at-home children a voice by developing substantive theories from an interpretivist approach (Denzin 1997; Yanow and Schwartz-Shea 2014), drawn from the grounded theory traditions (Glaser and Strauss 1967; Geertz 1973; Schwandt 1994). In the following section, I will, firstly, provide some background information about homework supervision in China to help the readers understand why the migrant parents are so eager to monitor their children's study from afar.

Parents and homework supervision in China

Supervising children's homework and caring about their exam marks at school constitutes an important part of parental responsibility in contemporary China (Zou, Anderson, and Tsey 2013). Studies show that Chinese parents not only have high expectations for their children's professional future and educational attainment, but are also highly involved in their children's education (Kipnis 2005; Obendiek 2016; Zhang 2020).

On the one hand, Chinese parents participate voluntarily because they believe education is the only way to help their children achieve security and success in marketized China (Doepke and Zilibotti 2019). To help their children seize the only chance they see, the parents engage in the children's study process intensively and push their children hard to study. On the other hand, the parents must get involved in their children's school education because schools nowadays shift much of their work to parents in the name of encouraging parent-child interactions at home.

The intensity of parental involvement in children's homework differs in the empirical cases. Here, I summarize the six tasks the parents perform in supervising the children's homework.

Parents' tasks of homework supervision		
	Interaction with the children	Interaction with the teacher	Frequency
1	(compulsory) Check whether the children have finished the written assignments on their own.	Teachers may call the parents if they did not check, and criticize them for being uncaring about and irresponsible for the child's study, future and well-being.	Daily
2	(compulsory) Check whether the children have finished the oral assignments (e.g. reading, reciting and mental calculation).	The parents need to record videos of children doing the oral assignments and upload the videos to the class's online chat group.	Daily
3	(compulsory) Review the child's exam paper. Note in their minds where the child lost points and give the child extra targeted practices.	The parents need to sign on the exam paper or send a message to the teacher to prove that they have reviewed the exam paper.	Bi-monthly for elementary school; monthly for junior high school; weekly for senior high school.
4	(compulsory) Cooperate with the child in certain kinds of homework assignments. Usually for lower grade students' parents. Exemplarily, preparing 1 kg rice for the child to bring to school to learn weight units; do paper cutting with the child.	Children usually cannot finish these homework assignments without the help of adults. If the parents do not participate, the teacher would criticize the parents publicly in the class's online chat group.	Three to five times a semester.
5	(compulsory or voluntary) Watch the children doing homework, mark the result and supervise the child correcting what is wrong.	When it is compulsory, the parents need to take pictures of the marked homework and upload it to the chat group.	Daily
6	(voluntary) Give extra homework to the children to either learn in advance or consolidate what has been learnt already.	Teachers would praise the parents' close supervision in the class's chat group, and encourage other parents to supervise closely as well. Teachers would also have a better impression of the child and the parents because they 'cooperate' well with the school education.	Daily

If the parents fail to finish the compulsory tasks, the teachers will, firstly, call the parents in private and persuade them to cooperate with the teachers at home. If they continue to ignore the children's homework, the teacher will name the parents in the class's online chat group and shame them as irresponsible and uncaring. Here is what a teacher writes in a class's WeChat group when a mother forgets to check and correct a child's homework.

> Teacher: @Jinghaoran Mom (Jinghaoran is the child's name) How busy were you during weekends? Do you care about your child? Last term your child scored 98 in the final exam, look at this assignment, how many marks can he get this time? A good child has been ruined like this by you!
> Teacher: @all parents I am so angry. I've posted the answers for reference in the chat group, but you just didn't look at it and correct your child's assignments. It is useless for the children to do exercises if you don't correct their exercises. Only if you mark what is wrong, will the teacher be able to see what the child has not mastered, so that we can target our teaching. How many hours a day does a teacher have to go through all the children's homework? I teach three classes this semester, I will need to correct assignments from 125 children every day. Is it possible? Think of it yourself. How can we do our job well, how can we help your children, if you, the parents, don't cooperate? Please invest your precious time in your children. A child's future is most valuable! Parents who have not corrected the homework should finish it tonight. Take pictures and upload them to the group.

According to this quote, the teaching activity of marking and correcting homework is defined as the parents' responsibility. The shift of responsibility is commonly reported in my conversations with other parent informants and has been reported many times in the news in China in the last few years. Marking homework is a vital part of teaching, as it helps the teachers adapt to the level of the students. However, as the teacher in the quote complains, her current teaching load is overwhelming, and she, thus, does not have time to check homework assignments carefully individually. The huge workload is commonly experienced by teachers in China. According to the National Education Development Statistics (2021), the teacher-student ratio in elementary school is 1:16.33, in junior high school 1:12.64 and in senior high school 1:12.84 in China (Ministry of Education of the People's Republic of China 2022). Although the ratio is similar to the Organisation for Economic Co-operation and Development's average, which is 1:14.4 at elementary school and 1:13.6 at secondary schools (OECD 2022), the teacher's workload can still be greater because of the longer teaching hours. According to the informants, the average teaching hours of elementary school lower grades are 910 hours, elementary school higher grades 1050 hours, junior high schools 1190 hours and senior high schools 1485 hours. By contrast, the teaching hours of the Organisation for Economic Co-operation and

Development's average are 885 hours at elementary schools and 776 hours at secondary schools (OECD 2022). Therefore, the teaching load for Chinese teachers is much greater, and they usually need to work overtime to finish all the tasks (and all the extra work is unpaid). To deal with the overwhelming work, many teachers have no choice but to shift the task of marking homework to the parents. However, teachers' huge workload is a result of structural and organizational dysfunction. Neither the teacher nor the parents should take responsibility for that. It is the education bureau and the schools that should hire more teachers to share the work burden. In the current situation, the unreasonable workload was solved by the free labour of the parents and the teachers, thus, making the education bureau and the school invisible in the negotiation.

In this quote, the child's poor homework quality and the decreased score are attributed to the parents' negligence. The wording in the quote is emotional abusive. The teacher tries to make the parents feel guilty for the child's school regression and challenges their self-perception as responsible caregivers. By shaming one mother publicly in the chat group, the teacher also exerts pressure on the other parents. In so doing, the teacher gradually transforms all parents into her obedient and cooperative partners. Furthermore, the idea that responsible and caring parents should closely engage in their children's school education and be responsible for their exam scores is reinforced during the process, forcing the parents to sacrifice their leisure time after work for the children's homework.

When parents naturize such morality, they begin to actively assign extra homework to their children to fulfil their parental responsibility. The close supervision is often effective and increases the child's exam score. The more the children practice at home, the better they can do at solving specific types of questions in exams. As the children make progress under close supervision, the parents also acquire a sense of accomplishment and become proud of their contribution. When the supervision is too detailed and the extra work given to the children is too much, the children can also develop an aversion to studying and, in extreme cases, refuse to study at all. When their efforts fail to help the children progress in their studies, parents can become exhausted and anxious. They complain about why their children are so 'disobedient' (不乖 *bu guai*), on the one hand, and are worried about the harsh competition their children might face in the job market in the future when they do not attain a tertiary education degree, on the other. Although close supervision of homework may cause intergenerational conflicts, all the parents I interviewed decided to adopt close homework supervision anyway. They all believed they knew their children the balance point and would stop before pushing the child to the limit.

Migrant parents and process of distant supervision via smart cameras

While most non-migrant parents can sit beside their children at night and watch them write in person, migrant parents rely heavily, if not entirely, on monitoring technologies to supervise their children's study after school. Smart cameras are one of the most popular devices migrant parents use to supervise their children's homework and tutor them from afar.

Picture 1: A smart camera standing on piles of tissue paper on the study desk on the left, and a screenshot of the livestreaming on the mother's phone on the right (photos taken in 2021 and are provided by Mrs Zheng to the author)

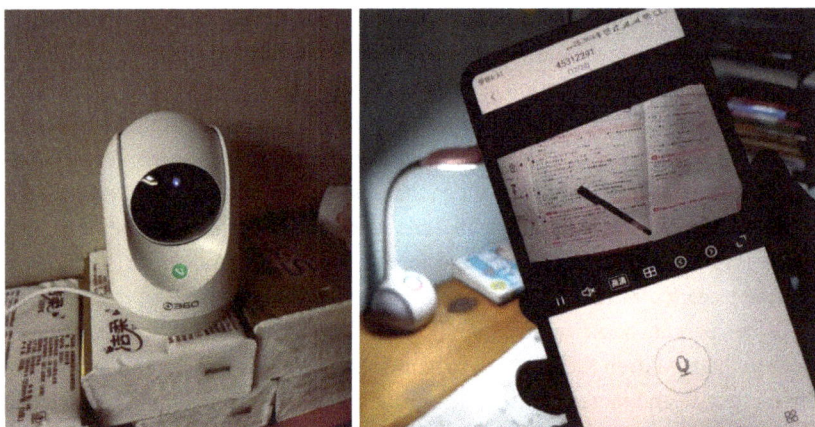

Mr and Mrs Zheng are migrant professionals in Hangzhou. The husband is a wealth planner, and the wife runs a bakery. To supervise their left-behind 12-year-old son's study at night, the couple installed a smart camera above his study desk, which is compounded with an ultra-high-definition camera, AI figure track, 360-degree panoramic view, and a two-way online phone call. The monitoring camera is linked to an app on the parent's smartphone, so the parent could control the recording view of the camera, view the livestream as well as the recorded video, and talk to the child with the phone.

The son promised the mother that he would study after school from 18:30 to 22:00 every weekday. In the first two hours, he needs to finish school assignments. In the following half hour, he needs to report to the mother via the camera about what he has studied during the day. In the final hour, the mother would, firstly, go through the school assignments with the son, making sure he had finished all the tasks. Then the mother would accompany the son while he did extra maths assignments from an unpublished exercise book edited by a famous teacher in Hangzhou.

After he finished the extra work, the mother would show him the right answer. If the son could not understand the problem-solving process, he needed to ask the maths teacher the day after because the mother was unable to tutor him anymore as he moved to junior high school.

The time frame between 18:30 and 20:30 is a busy hour for bakeries in China, as many people buy cakes and bread as desserts to take home after work. Thus, during the first two hours, the mother usually relies on the AI report produced by the smart camera to monitor the child's homework writing process. Smart cameras nowadays are equipped with AI image processing technologies and can provide real-time analysis to the smartphone. The reports shows up as notice banners on the smartphone in short sentences that indicate the time point at which the son shows up in or leaves the room. When he comes and goes, the AI would also calculate how long he stayed or was absent. Accordingly, the mother could track the son's movements even without logging into the app and checking the livestreaming video on her own.

The time after involves higher levels of interpersonal communication as the number of customers reduces by 20:30 and the mother can finally take a rest after a long day of work. The mother and son go through school assignments together and discuss school life as if they were sitting in one room and sharing the moment face-to-face. The camera becomes an external eye and mouth for the mother, enabling her to see, communicate and interact with him across geographical distance. Although very tired, the mother insists on meeting with her son via the camera to check his homework.

In addition to the real-time mediated gathering via the camera, Mr and Mrs Zheng love to review their son's study videos during the day when they are not busy. The camera can upload the video to the cloud, where it will be stored for three days. The couple downloaded many of the son's studying videos locally on the phone and watch them again and again when they feel tired at work. Mrs Zheng once told me that "Everyone in the family works hard for a better life. Life is hard for everyone, but I am happy that my family is so united. I believe our days will get better and better." The mother felt relieved every time she watched her son study hard and the husband brings money back. Here, they also constitute a spatially dispersed parent-child striving team, a notion coined by sociologist Rachel Murphy (2020). Based on long-term field work in middle China, Murphy argues that the migrant parents and the left-behind children live their lives interdependently, and all contribute their hard work to the family goal of striving for a better life. The migrants' labour in the cities and the children's study in their hometowns are all real work that is underpinned by aspirations to bring about a better life for the family members. The idea of a striving team helps us to understand Mr and Mrs Zheng's relief when they saw their son's studying video. Studying hard is the son's way to contribute to the family's well-being and increase the family's social mobility. When the parents watch the son's study video, they also feel they are supported by the son, and the responsibility to make the family better is shared by him. This experience of cooperation creates a sense of togetherness and strengthens the bonds between the family members without requiring them to be physically close.

The experience of family communication via monitoring camera from the perspective of the left-behind son is more complex and mixed. The son, for example, hates the camera, but, at the same time, he is so reliant on the camera to give him a sense of being kept in his parents' heart and being missed. The son compared himself with his friends, who were also left-behind children but had been forgotten by their migrant parents. He concluded that his parents installed cameras on his study table to supervise his studies, ensure he was doing the right thing at the right time, and be accountable to him. As this boy lives far away from his parents and craves their attention, being monitored gives him the feeling of being loved and cared for.

In addition, the camera is the only direct way he could contact the parents. He does not have a mobile phone, because his parents are afraid that he might be distracted from studying and waste time on games on the phone. Thus, he needs the camera to contact his parents on his own. Although the boy has thought of uninstalling the camera several times, he has never once implemented this plan up to the date I talked to him. At the end of our conversation, the boy defined his temptation to remove the camera as an immature and impetuous thought and said: "The monitor does help me with my studies. [Long pause] It gives my parents reassurance. I guess it's the only way for me to show my filial piety at my age."

Not every child I encounter in China thinks like this boy. There were also children who attempted to break the camera and those who tried to hide from the camera by stacking books like a wall and hiding behind the books. But what is the same among these children is their mixed perception of the parents' distant monitoring practice. No matter how obedient or rebellious the children behave, all of them share a mixed feeling in the monitoring relationship, on the one hand, feeling cared about and, on the other hand, feeling distrusted. Surveillance is intimately entangled with care and love in the situation of parental migration and children staying at home. Smart cameras extend the parents' authoritative watch across time and space and enable careful surveillance that is both loving and scary in the eyes of the children. I will investigate this complexity in the following section through concepts of 'forced' and 'uncertain co-presence'.

Forced co-presence rooted in an unequal parent-child power relationship

The children feel uncomfortable with the camera-facilitated distant homework supervision because they have lost control over their own presence. The use of smart cameras generates what I call 'forced co-presence', which depicts an unequal power relationship between the migrant parents and their stay-at-home children.

The story of Zheng's family shows that the stay-at-home son is forced to livestream his study to the migrant parents every day. He does not like doing homework under his parents' supervision for two main reasons. On the one hand, he has lost autonomy over his own time under smart monitoring. He cannot, for example, stop studying at night without parental permission. When he could not stay focused on study, the boy could not go directly to the bed and lie down for a while. Instead, he needs to press the talking button on the camera and report his tiredness to his parents and ask for a rest. If he stopped studying without a report in advance, he would be scolded or nagged about it repeatedly as soon as the parents found out from the recorded video. In order to get moments of respite, the boy has now learnt to take a secret rest by staring blankly at the exercise book and pretending to encounter and think about a difficult question. Deception is the only means that enables him to take back control of his own time, but, in the meantime, it often makes him feel immoral. He felt guilty for lying to his parents and being irresponsible in his own study. This is how he comments on his little trick:

> My parents work hard outside to save money for my future education. I need to repay (报答baoda) them by studying hard. The hardship of studying is nothing compared to the hardship they go through in making money outside. I feel so angry why I can't learn all the time like the top students in my class. Believe it or not, I feel guilty regarding my parents when I pretend to study. I also know I do not study for my parents or for the teacher, I study for myself. So, it made me feel worse.

On the other hand, the boy felt distrusted by his parents during close homework supervision. At the time of the interview, the boy was thirteen years old and complained that his parents still supervised him like a preschool child. His development is constantly ignored by his parents and they often take away any credit for his study progress. He said hatefully:

> I can study well without their supervision. I can do it myself. I don't need their so-called help. I will finish the homework without their supervision, and I can ask the teachers about the questions I don't understand. Why can't they leave me alone and let me be responsible for my own study?

The boy's experience resonates with many other children who are similarly supervised closely by their parents, whether distantly or in person. The parents check the children's homework and make sure they finished it correctly and well every night because they do not trust their children. They despise their children's self-management skills and ability to take the initiative in studying. As a result, these parents are always eager to become overly involved in their children's education.

Distant but close homework supervision in China is enabled by cheap and easily accessible smart cameras. A decade ago, migrant parents were technically unable to overparent their stay-at-home children across long distances. In the age of internet video calls and phone calls, children have the right to refuse the chat invitation at the beginning or hang up the phone when they no longer want to communicate. When the parents ask about their refusal, the children could make excuses about an unstable connection, being out of battery, and so on and so forth. In an earlier era of letter exchange, children could refuse more easily by writing shorter and less frequently to their parents. Nowadays, in cases of smart camera monitoring, the children do not have any excuse for refusing to be monitored. Firstly, the monitors are usually hung high on the wall or in the ceiling, making it impossible for small children to uninstall the camera. Even if they uninstall it, the grandparents who reside with them will reinstall it quickly on behalf of the parents. Secondly, the monitors work 24/7, and whenever the children enter the space of surveillance, their image is captured and transmitted immediately to the cloud. The children have no access to editing or deleting the videos. Of course, the children could break the monitor, but it would be at the expense of irritating the migrant parents, failing to complete certain types of homework and being chastised by teachers at school, as many pieces of homework should be completed in collaboration with the parents, as discussed in the preceding section. The emergence of smart monitoring signals a retreat in intergenerational equality, because parents are technically able to force their children to listen to their nagging and stay monitored at a low cost, such as in face-to-face situations.

Uncertain co-presence determined by data synchronization

The co-presence facilitated by smart cameras is as uncertain as Schrödinger's cat. The state of the co-presence is measured until the parents synchronize with the camera as they review the recorded video or read the message transmitted by the AI to their phone. Children cannot determine whether they are being watched or not by their parents when the former are doing homework. The camera-mediated co-presence exists in two states before the human-machine data synchronization, like the cat being both dead and alive before the box is opened in Schrödinger's famous thought experiment. By contrast, other forms of co-presence are more definite in generating a sense of togetherness. Physical co-presence, for example, is multi-sensational and can, thus, be clearly perceived by seeing, hearing or smelling. As for ambient co-presence in a polymedia environment (Madianou 2016), although the sense of togetherness is peripheral, individuals can perceive the presence of the distant other by seeing them put up new posts or noticing the little green dot near their profile photo, which indicates that the friend is online. People would not question whether they shared the moment with other people on social media.

Compared with a definite experience of togetherness, the co-presence experience mediated by smart cameras is ambiguous for interactants. When the parents told the children they should be away for a while and come back later, the children could not determine whether they were still under their parents' watch as the camera continued to record, livestream and store the video. The camera functions as a loosely connected external eye and external brain for the parents. It is loosely connected because the linkage depends on the parents' intentional acts of data synchronization. In the case of distant homework supervision, it can either refer to the migrant parents reviewing the video on the cloud or reading the AI report on their phone later. Therefore, the migrant parents are both present and absent before they retrieve data from the camera. The interaction of watching and being watched, as well as the state of co-presence which took place at a prior time, are dependent on the act of parent-camera synchronization, which happens later. In this sense, it is very difficult for the children to perceive and experience co-presence with the parents at the exact moment of doing their homework under the camera.

This delayed certainty, which can be perplexing for the children being monitored, has significant negative emotional consequences for distant parent-child relationships, on the one hand, and lowers study productivity, on the other. According to interviews and informal conversations with the children, when they are unsure whether their parents are watching them, they become more anxious and less focused. They have wasted a lot of time guessing what their parents are doing, and are less able to concentrate on their homework. A nine-year-old girl shared her experience as follows:

> She [the migrant mother] sometimes leaves without noticing me when I am doing homework. She always tells me she doesn't reply to me when I talk to her on purpose. Because she wanted to see if I could concentrate on my work when she is absent. I don't know if she was telling a lie. She can always check the video afterwards and tell me she was there. She could watch the monitoring video and pretend to be with me. I cannot stop talking to her to get feedback from her. She complains that I talk too much while doing homework. But I just want to make sure she is there. She doesn't understand me. She just criticizes me.

In camera-mediated homework supervision, the migrant parents can see and hear what the children are doing from the livestreaming video, but the stay-at-home children cannot see the migrant parents. They need to confirm the presence of their parents by talking to and hearing from them. The quality and quantity of information exchanged between the monitor and the monitored are unequal. The parents are so privileged that they often cannot understand the children's needs for confirming their co-presence. In this story, the mother takes the girl's attempt to seek confirmation of her presence as evidence of study wandering and criticizes the girl for not being focused on study. The girl feels wronged and misunderstood by her mother. Following the expression of grievance, the girl continued to share her complaints about her mother.

> Talking does distract me from my homework. I agree. But I feel more uncomfortable and more distracted if I fail to get her response. When I receive her response, I feel so relieved and assured, and can go back to study immediately. So, my talking is not problem. Her not replying makes me unconcentrated.

The girl's complaint reveals a strong sense of insecurity about the long-distance parent-child relationship. Homework time was the only moment she could share with her mother for the day. She needs a definite sense of the mother's presence to perceive and confirm the mother's love and care for her. She needs the mother's full attention and, thus, feels anxious when the mother does not reply to her. The longer she experiences silence, the more she suffers from anxiety.

The 'uncertain co-presence' also has consequences for children's understandings of the human-machine relationship. When I watched the monitoring video posts on Weibo, I found preschool children often mixed up their parents with the monitoring camera. In one video, when a little boy fell while going up the steps between the yard and the house, he looked up and cried to the monitoring camera at the entrance: "Daddy I fell, I'm in pain, Daddy, Daddy......" This video has been widely distributed on Weibo and has aroused a strong sense of compassion for the left-behind children. Children at a young age could not discern humans from machines as they have been used to talking to the camera. This little boy thought the monitoring camera was his father and could comfort him and help him up when he fell. The boy thought the father saw his fall from the camera and would react to him immediately; however, the father could only see the whole process when he reviewed the recorded video late at night after work. The camera is more than a proxy in Baldassar's theory of proxy-co-presence; it is tangible and incorporates the spirit of the absent father. The camera is also interactive and smart, giving the child the illusion that it is not only an object but a technical extension of the human father. The boy is disappointed and cries hard when the camera – in his understanding, it is his father – does not respond to him. In another story shared on Xiaohongshu, a mother reported that her three-year-old daughter was angry with her migrant father when the daughter offered a piece of apple to the monitoring camera but the camera did not take it. People found this episode 'so funny' because good comedy is tragic at its core. The story is so sad because the girl could not distinguish the father from the camera, as the father always appears in the form of a voice from the camera. In the eyes of the little girl, the camera is the father, and the father is the camera. She expected the camera to interact with her and take her apple, as the mother always does in these situations. Such disappointment is increasingly commonly experienced by small stay-at-home children in contemporary China raised under monitoring cameras.

Conclusion

In this chapter, I have documented the use of smart cameras in distant homework supervision among translocal families in Eastern China. The ethnographic details show how education aspiration, parental responsibility and the school system interact to push the parents to be highly involved in their children's homework and study. In such a context, migrant parents should rely on technologies to recreate translocal spaces for homework supervision to fulfil their parental responsibilities and explore new ways of 'doing parent' at a distance.

However, the use of smart cameras deprived the stay-at-home children of the right to control their own presence and brought about what I call 'forced co-presence', which is deeply rooted in the unequal parent-child power relationship. Children have no other choice but to use lies to take back their time for rest under their parents' micromanagement. The moral uneasiness of deception decreases the mental wellbeing of children and undeniably harms their intimate relationships. Furthermore, the use of smart cameras creates uncertainty about the state of co-presence. Without knowing whether the parents retrieve the data from the camera afterwards, the children cannot confirm whether they have been carefully monitored by the parents from afar. The uncertainty generates the children's need for immediate confirmation of their parents' invisible presence during the homework writing. It distracts them from concentrating on their studies and lowers their study efficiency.

I argue that the use of smart cameras makes the stay-at-home children insecure and feel untrusted. While close homework supervision eases migrant parents' anxiety over their children's study performance, it might also weaken the parent-child relationship at a distance. Therefore, the distant homework supervision I studied in this chapter highlights the precarious balance between responsible parenting and overparenting. It also expands on the concept of co-presence and sheds light on the effects of technology on translocal and transnational family relationship formation in digital and mobile societies. As smart monitoring was widely used in child and elderly care in many societies around the world during and after the COVID-19 pandemic, the terms 'forced co-presence' and 'uncertain co-presence' help us to see that smart monitoring has ambiguous consequences for 'doing family' at a distance.

Bibliography

Alinejad, Donya. 2019. "Careful Co-presence: The Transnational Mediation of Emotional Intimacy." *Social Media + Society* 5 (2). https://doi.org/10.1177/205630511985 4222.

Baldassar, Loretta. 2008. "Missing Kin and Longing to be Together: Emotions and the Construction of Co-presence in Transnational Relationships." *Journal of Intercultural Studies* 29 (3): 247–66. https://doi.org/10.1080/07256860802169196.

———. 2016. "De-demonizing Distance in Mobile Family Lives: Co-presence, Care Circulation and Polymedia as Vibrant Matter." *Global Networks* 16: 145–63. https://doi.org/10.1111/glob.12109.

Carsten, Janet, ed. 2000. *Cultures of Relatedness: New Approaches to the Study of Kinship.* Oxford: Oxford University Press.

Chen, Feinian, Guangya Liu, and Christine A. Mair. 2011. "Intergenerational Ties in Context: Grandparents Caring for Grandchildren in China." *Social Forces* 90: 571–594. https://doi.org/10.1093/sf/sor012.

Chong, Gladys Pak Lei. 2022. "Xiaomi and the Promises of the Good Life? Issues of Security and Risk in the Making of the Smart Home in China." *Science, Technology and Society* 28 (1). https://doi.org/10.1177/0971721822107512.

Denzin, Norman K. 1997. *Interpretive Ethnography: Ethnographic Practices for the 21st Century.* Thousand Oaks; London; New Delhi: Sage Publications.

Doepke, Matthias, and Fabrizio Zilibotti. 2019. *Love, Money, and Parenting: How Economics Explains the Way We Raise Our Kids.* Princeton and Oxford: Princeton University Press.

Finch, Janet. 2007. "Displaying Families." *Sociology* 41 (1): 65–81. https://doi.org/10.1177/0038038507072284.

Geertz, Clifford. 1973. *The Interpretation of Cultures: Selected Essays.* New York: Basic Books.

Glaser, Barney, and Anselm Strauss. 1967. *The Discovery of Grounded Theory: Strategies for Qualitative Research.* Chicago, IL: Aldine.

Goffman, Erving. 1983. "The Interaction Order: American Sociological Association, 1982 Presidential Address." *American Sociological Review* 48 (1). https://doi.org/10.2307/2095141.

Kipnis, Andrew B. 2005. *Governing Educational Desire: Culture, Politics and Schooling in China.* Chicago: University of Chicago Press.

Li, Zhen. 2017. "'天网'加'雪亮'　城乡共平安." 人民日报 *China Daily*), October 17, 2017. Accessed 16.02.2023. https://web.archive.org/web/202006120 62420/http://webcache.googleusercontent.com/search?q=cache%3AtlxGtyKqbl 4J%3Apaper.people.com.cn%2Frmrbhwb%2Fhtml%2F2017-10%2F11%2Fconten t_1809752.htm+&cd=2&hl=en&ct=clnk&gl=us.

Madianou, Mirca. 2016. "Ambient Co-presence: Transnational Family Practices in Polymedia Environments." *Global Networks* 16 (2): 183–201. https://doi.org/10.11 11/glob.12105.

Madianou, Mirca, and Daniel Miller. 2012. "Polymedia: Towards a New Theory of Digital Media in Interpersonal Communication." *International Journal of Cultural Studies* 16 (2): 169–87. https://doi.org/10.1177/1367877912452486.

Ministry of Education of the People's Republic of China. 2022. *National Education Development Statistics 2021.* http://www.moe.gov.cn/jyb_sjzl/sjzl_fztjgb/202209/t2 0220914_660850.html.

Montanari, Giulia, and Tino Schlinzig. 2022. "Family and Space – an Interpretive Perspective on Two Central Concepts in Population Geography." *Geographica Helvetica* 77 (2): 255–62. https://doi.org/10.5194/gh-77-255-2022.

Morgan, David H. J. 2011. *Rethinking Family Practices.* London: Palgrave Macmillan UK.

Murphy, Rachel. 2020. *The Children of China's Great Migration.* Cambridge University Press.

Nedelcu, Mihaela, and Malika Wyss. 2016. "'Doing Family' through ICT-mediatedordinary Ordinary Co-presence: Transnational Communication Practices of Romanian Migrants in Switzerland." *Global Networks* 16 (2): 202–18. https://doi.org /10.1111/glob.12110.

Obendiek, Helena. 2016. *"Changing Fate": Education, Poverty and Family Support in Contemporary Chinese Society.* Berlin: LIT.

OECD: Organisation for Economic Co-operation and Development. 2022. *Education at a Glance 2022: OECD Indicators.* Paris: OECD Publishing.

Sahlins, Marshall. 2013. *What Kinship Is – And Is Not.* Chicago, Ill.: University of Chicago Press.

Schütz, Alfred, and Thomas Luckmann. 1974. *The Structures of the Life-World.* Vol. 1. Translated by Richard M. Zaner and H. Tristram Engelhardt. London: Heinemann Educational Books.

Schwandt, Thomas A. 1994. "Constructivist, Interpretivist Approaches to Human Inquiry." In *Handbook of Qualitative Research,* edited by Norman K. Denzin and Yvonna S. Lincoln, 118–37. Thousand Oaks: Sage.

Strathern, Marilyn. 1992. *Reproducing the Future: Essays on Anthropology, Kinship and the New Reproductive Technologies.* Manchester: Manchester University Press.

Yanow, Dvora, and Peregrine Schwartz-Shea. 2014. *Interpretation and Method: Empirical Research Methods and the Interpretive Turn.* 2 ed. London and New York: Routledge.

Zhang, Wei. 2020. "Shadow Education in the Service of Tiger Parenting: Strategies Used by Middle-class Families in China." *European Journal of Education* 55 (3): 388–404. https://doi.org/10.1111/ejed.12414.

Zou, Wuying, Neil Anderson, and Komla Tsey. 2013. "Middle-class Chinese Parental Expectations for Their Children's Education." *Procedia – Social and Behavioral Sciences* 106: 1840–9. https://doi.org/10.1016/j.sbspro.2013.12.209.

The Class Diary of the Pandemic. Comics of the Transformations of the 'Presence' in Brazilian Schools during the COVID-19 Pandemic

João Pedro Rangel Gomes da Silva and Matheus Fred Schulze

Abstract *The Class Diary is a lecture tool for registering the daily routine and the presence of students. In 2020 and 2021, we ethnographically investigated the transformations brought about by the pandemic through the stories of those particularly affected in the educational context: teachers and students. These stories were collected and illustrated as a diary that anthropologically explores the experience of having new ways of 'presence' in the pandemic.*

Each story has their own particularities but together they are crossed by interconnected experiences and sensations. The fear of the present shares space with the hope of change in the future. We were interested in the transformations that arose in teacher-student relations – at that moment exclusively online ones – that resulted in a new mode of 'presence' of these subjects, and consequently, a new way of experiencing their senses and the establishment of relationships.

By appropriating the notion of Class Diary for the record of daily presence, we explored these records and transformed them into illustrations to sensitively comprehend and express this new sense of 'presence' experienced by our interlocutors. A virtual and everyday presence. A way of experiencing different moments, previously physically present, but now in an online environment. The Class Diary is seen as a registration of stories, feelings, and the relationships between these subjects. But how to represent hope in the future, if the future was extremely uncertain to those facing that moment? Our challenge was to transform these stories into a comic book, without missing the point of view of our interlocutors and the miscellaneous senses that crossed them, seeking ways of expressing it artistically.

Keywords *Comics; Pandemic; Education; Presence*

Introduction

Programa de Extensão em Educação Política (PROEEP)[1] is an outreach program[2] in Political Education that aims to develop and disseminate educational content on politics, enabling people of all ages to participate in public life. Our group was created in 2019 as an initiative of undergraduate and master's students of the Institute of Philosophy and Human Sciences of the Universidade Estadual de Campinas (UNICAMP), in a partnership with the Legislative Branch's School of Campinas, Brazil (ELECAMP). In this project, we carry out activities in the Youth Parliament, an initiative that receives elementary and high school students from public and private schools from all municipalities to simulate sessions of the city's legislative body. The students learn about all the processes within that space, from the creation of a bill to voting.

By the end of 2019, the project was fully linked to the partnership with the legislative body, but in the following year (2020) we could start executing different plans and ideas. However, with the pandemic, all these plans had to be changed, and the physical presence had to be transformed completely. The project migrated to the online environment, and we had to adapt to this new type of work and think about what we would do from there onwards since our main activity, the Youth Parliament, was paralyzed.

Therefore, we increased our content production for social networks, such as posts explaining some concepts and indicating artworks, books, and documentaries to help people think about political themes. We produced online courses and classes, prepared two board games about the Brazilian legislative process and a booklet about the elections in the country. Finally, during this period, we produced two editions of "The Class Diary of the Pandemic" book, which will be the theme of this paper.[3]

PROEEP is built by undergraduate, master's, and doctoral students from Unicamp, assembling various professional and training experiences. During the pandemic, we were included in a privileged space of one of the best universities in Latin America and faced several obstacles generated by the transfer of traditional face-to-face teaching to distance learning. These changes entailed profound transformations in several layers of our experience as university students, something that can

---

1   PROEEP's social networks, productions, and work are available here: https://linktr.ee/PROE EP
2   Outreach, alongside teaching and research, constitutes the three pillars of Brazilian public universities. The particularity of the outreach programs is the exchange of knowledge and collaboration between the university community and external society.
3   They are not published yet. The first edition of The Class Diary of the Pandemic is available here: https://drive.google.com/file/d/1gar2omXHq5Z61Yj2OLEEn4PeV7-01NM_/view?usp=s hare_link

be felt and made sense through our bodies, which had to suddenly adapt to a teaching-learning model that we were not used to. The consequences of these transformations are something that we seek to investigate through the reports of students and teachers of different levels of education. The impact of the pandemic was different across Brazilian institutions, and our university had more resources than other smaller educational institutions.

The notions of time and space gained other nuances due to the dynamics of distance learning. We no longer had the commute to the university, the conversations in the corridors, the interactions in the classroom, the coffee breaks, the schedules, and the traditional evaluation methods. In the online study environment, where we had to be present at distance, technical problems were common, fatigue became generalized by the hours on end in front of screens, as well as pain from sitting too long in front of a computer. The teaching-learning space suffered the most significant change, as there was no longer a physical place to go to and live our student life. The boundaries between home and the university/school space have become blurred over time. This blurring happened not only in our university experience but also in the reports of many students and teachers living this period. With these transformations, social inequalities among students became even more evident. Some had all the gadgets and features they needed to comfortably carry on with the school year at home, but for many, there was a lack of internet, a computer, study space, and food.

As humanities students, these elements already caught our attention before, but we became even more interest when we were taking the place of teachers. In our education path at Unicamp, we can follow different areas, Anthropology, Sociology, Political Science, a bachelor's degree and or a teaching degree. Thus, some of our members were experiencing all this change from two different spectra: as a student and a teacher.

Our initial curiosity took the form of a desire to record what we did not see being registered. In the beginning, we looked for references, whether or not they were produced, and we came across materials that documented life stories of people who died of COVID-19. However, we wanted to make room for the stories of people living during the pandemic, more specifically teachers in elementary and high school.

We made an open call for reports to the project we called "The Class Diary of the Pandemic". What is a class diary? A class diary is a document used by teachers in the classroom, where they record the life and dynamics of that space, including the presence and participation of students and lesson planning. Thus, through these day-to-day reports during an unprecedented social-political scenario, we aimed to understand the changes and permanent situations from the perception of these individuals. We perceived something we felt in our own experiences regarding the notion of presence: what was considered to be present before was no longer possible in a period of social isolation.

Given the health and political emergency of the pandemic, we realized the importance of thoroughly investigating the experiences of those deeply affected individuals and the consequences for teaching, which cannot be understood until this day. Thus, we are guided by the observation and description of these stories, through processes of experimentation and sensitization with different modes of expression (text, sound, images, comics). We searched for details and connections of this experience with what is beyond it, although it does not seem so at first. Our goal was to leave the experience and go to the artistic expression of these stories, to allow the understanding of this historical moment.

On June 9, 2020, we launched our open call and contacted our network of acquaintances to collect these reports. The questions that guided these conversations included: Teacher, are you working through distance learning?; What digital platforms and lesson formats have you adopted?; How have students received them?; Have you adapted the topics in the classroom to address issues related to Covid-19? Which ones?; What challenges has the pandemic brought to the realization of your teaching work, inside and outside the classroom?

The answers that came to these questions were the most diverse and came in different formats. Some teachers felt more comfortable sending audio files, others preferred video files, and others sent texts. These open questions also provoked a reaction that we did not expect, which ended up bringing consequences to the development of the project. While some reports came full of details, others were very succinct and direct.

Another important point was the identity of these interlocutors. As they were active teachers, many of them felt more comfortable using pseudonyms to avoid any complications with their educational institutions; after all, their reports showed asymmetrical power relations between teachers, parents and the managers from the schools, conflicts, and criticism of the positions adopted by the schools. Aside from the pseudonyms, in some cases we needed to change the physical appearance of the characters, who, as a form of registration and as a tribute, were illustrated based on the actual participants. This request for anonymity appeared when we introduced the invitation to participate, a fact that made us add the possibility of anonymity to the other public calls we would post in our networks. An example of this is the report by teacher Maria Luiza, who requested the use of a pseudonym and a different representation in the drawings. She informed us that she preferred to remain anonymous for fear of being fired or having problems with the school.

The fear that the teachers shared with us is not banal. This feeling must be observed within the historical processes that Brazil has been through until today. The rise of a fascist and military government shortly before the pandemic in Brazil contributed to the establishment of a set of economic, political, social, and health crises with the arrival of the pandemic. In this context, there was a brutal deepening of social inequality, the establishment of genocidal policies by the federal government, devaluation of teachers, a drastic reduction in funding at all levels of education, and the return of Brazil to the hunger map, among many other aspects that generated acute insecurity among us and our interlocutors.[4]

Our idea was to collect the reports, illustrate them, and then post them on our social networks, as a sequence of images that referred to each story. However, shortly before finishing this process, we were faced with the opportunity to launch them in book format, which led to adaptations to produce a comic book. This adaptation process will be better covered in the next section but mentioning this change is crucial to understand the choices we made in the construction of the second edition.

On 1 June 2021, we opened a call for submissions of reports to the second The Class Diary of the Pandemic. In this edition, we aimed to tell the stories of students in the ninth grade of elementary school, high school, college prep school, and adult education. This time, however, the collection method was different: we organized a form that should be completed by the student with some personal data, authorizations, contacts of their legal guardians, and a series of questions regarding the experience of students in the pandemic.

The construction of this form went through several stages because it would invite people of different ages. It had to be understandable and, at the same time, have a logic structure of questions – which were open and free – to ensure clear communication and wealth of details. The questions were the following: How did you feel when the pandemic began?; How has your daily routine been? How is school part of your routine?; What moments of face-to-face teaching do you not find in distance learning? What do you miss?; Tell us a memory or a story of yours about online teaching. When the pandemic is over, what do you think you will remember the most?; Which class do you most like to attend? Why?; Which class do you least like to attend? Why? Do you have access difficulties? How is the internet access at your home? Do you have a cell phone? Do you have a computer? What changes and difficulties have you experienced with the transition to online teaching?; How do you feel about your school, your friends, and your teachers? Has this relationship changed with the

---

4   All these socio-political transformations can be seen in these newspaper articles: Alves, Lise. 2021. "Pandemic puts Brazil back on the world hunger map." The New Humanitarian, July 19, 2021. https://www.thenewhumanitarian.org/news-feature/2021/7/19/pandemic-puts-brazil-back-on-the-world-hunger-map; Lino Gomes, Nilma. 2020. "Racismo e novo coronavírus: armas mortíferas no Brasil." Nexo Jornal, July 4, 2020. https://www.nexojornal.com.br/ensaio/debate/2020/Racismo-e-novo-coronav%C3%ADrus-armas-mort%C3%ADferas-no-Brasil; Ramírez Ramos, María Fernanda. 2023. "Genocide Of the Yanomami People in Brazil: An Announced Tragedy Involving Bolsonaro." LatinAmerika Post, February 2, 2023. https://latinamericanpost.com/43344-genocide-of-the-yanomami-people-in-brazil-an-ann ounced-tragedy-involving-bolsonaro; Rodrigues, Meghie. 2021. "Scientists reel as Brazilian government backtracks on research funds." Nature, October 22, 2021. https://www.nature.c om/articles/d41586-021-02886-9.

pandemic?; If you could leave a message for your future self about the learnings and discoveries you had during the pandemic, what would it be?; If you were to illustrate yourself, how would you draw yourself? (For example, curly hair, glasses, brown eyes, etc.); If you were to create a character based on yourself, what would his/her name be?

Furthermore, we organized workshops entitled 'Build this diary', where we presented the first edition of The Class Diary of the Pandemic, followed by a discussion about the importance of diaries and their place as historical records. In the workshops, we used Anne Franks (1952) "The Diary of a Young Girl" and the book by Carolina Maria de Jesus (1963) "Child of the Dark: The Diary of Carolina Maria de Jesus". The two diaries were selected as a reference because they have comic versions. In the activity, we used other materials of this genre, but we took these two as our main focus because they dialogue more directly with our work, both in the narrative genre and in the media used for its presentation.

The workshops were open for the community and happened in virtual spaces such as high school virtual classrooms and live broadcasts in Unicamp's event calendar, the Unicamp Open House (UPA)[5]. The main objective of these workshops was to present the reflections we developed throughout the construction of the first book and idealization of the second and to encourage students to participate and send their reports. By arguing about the importance of the record of a historical moment, we wanted them to understand the importance of their daily experiences and feel motivated to participate.

The result of this work, combined with the growth of the project on social networks and an increase in the number of partnerships, led to a much larger number of people and attracted more reports. While in the first edition we had 13 reports, in the second we received 136, of which we selected 13. The selection was made by the illustrators based on previous experience and the proposals established for the book. They selected some questions from the questionnaire in which the answers best dialogued with the proposal; then, those that presented distinct realities and perceptions among reports were selected so that we could represent heterogeneous experiences within an already selected group.

Unlike the first, which gathered the reports as individual stories, the idea of the second book was to build a narrative that connected the stories. Thus, our protagonists would be in the future doing a job of revisiting the past to understand the transformations caused by the pandemic in social life. They would do this through

---

5   UPA is an annual event organized by Unicamp. In it, each institute of the university offers a special program to receive the general public. This program consists of activities prepared by the students and aims to present what is produced inside the university. One of the main focuses is to show high school students how the courses work, what is taught, etc. so that they can decide on the courses they intend to take in the future.

the reports and, as a consequence, show the similarities and differences of realities experienced during the same period, recorded by different individuals. Above all, this is an important historical record of our time, including the dynamics and political and social relationships involved in the experience of these subjects.

Two authors are crucial to comprehend our work, Merleau Ponty and Georges Didi-Huberman. Both address how we access the world through our bodies crossed by our emotions in this process.

Merleau Ponty (2004) in his lectures builds reflections on embodiment and how we access the world. He shows that there isn't a division between body and mind, emotion and reason. Merleau Ponty indicates that our access to the world is embodied – we are our senses, we don't use our senses. His reflections are important to think about what happens when students are obligated to interact only through videos, in the destitution of interaction moments related to day-to-day life in the classroom teaching-learning environment. This radical change is implicated in different embodied experiences, emotions, and sensations. This new experience is what we explored in our work.

Didi-Huberman (2016) makes a historical approach to how emotions in intellectual and philosophical history were faced as a demonstration of weakness, flaw, and powerlessness. From Plato to Kant, emotions are opposed to reason, and most of these philosophers considered reason the best thing. According to Didi-Huberman, emotions would also be opposed to action making a triple impasse: language impasse, emotional I became mute; Thought impasse, emotional I lose my references; Action impasse, emotional I cannot move. These intellectuals criticized emotions as something negative. In our project, we sought through these reports to comprehend what was being experienced during the pandemic, something that is intrinsically embodied and felled through our interlocutor's senses and emotions.

Didi-Huberman proposes to rethink the opposition between action and passion. For him, emotions are not only producers of an impasse but active gestures that provoke and move us. In this sense, emotions are movements and actions, a sensible knowledge capable of changing. Mobilizing Merleau Ponty, Didi-Huberman (2016, 28) explains: "It is an affective movement that 'owns' us, but which we do not 'possess' entirely since it is largely unknown to us".

We sought to appropriate these reports and transform them into comics. So, we could express how our interlocutors were being crossed by the pandemic. Which meant getting closer to their emotions and how this process happened through their bodies.

Comics

During the idealization period of The Class Diary of the Pandemic project, we thought of some ways to express the stories we were interested in accessing and sharing. We started looking for references in May 2020 and came across several artistic productions, among them the Instagram account @reliquia.rum – which collected reports from family members of COVID-19 victims and made collages that represented those victims – and a book that gathered drawings by various artists about the experience in the pandemic. These references shaped both the idea of the project to collect reports and the way it would be presented. However, we believe that one of these references played a more significant role.

One of the most striking elements of this whole process was the fact that we, as researchers, were also experiencing the pandemic at the same time we were presenting other people's accounts of it. One of the illustrators, for example, began to do this type of art during the pandemic, since he inserted himself more deeply into the world of comics during the isolation period. This approach to comics also led him to read the comic version of Anne Franks "The Diary of a Young Girl" and this was the work that most inspired us to turn our stories into an illustrated series.

Comics and the process of drawing are a powerful medium. Nowadays, several productions have explored the many possibilities they offer. In anthropology itself, or the humanities, it is already possible to see a series of works in comics and also those that use the medium as a way of presenting themselves.[6]

In our view, the richness of this medium is in the infinity of possibilities generated by the combination of text and image; after all, even the absence of them can express different meanings on a page. Sylvia Caiuby Novaes (2014) writes about the power that photography and narrative would have to embrace experience if people contemplated and listened to them, respectively. We can transpose this reflection to comics when we think about the power of images allied to a narrative that, at the same time, guides the reader and invites them to interpret the message.

In 2014, Art Spiegelman, author and artist of "Maus: A Survivor's Tale" (1986), presented a lecture at Harvard's Sanders Theatre titled "What the %@&*! Happened

6   In the 2020 edition of the European Association of Social Anthropologists (EASA), two laboratories explored the relations between drawing and anthropology. The Laboratory "Drawing as Anthropology-Making" was about the use of comics in research, whose speakers, Letizia Bonanno (University of Kent) and José Sherwood Gonzalez (Manchester Metropolitan University), produced their dissertations in the format of graphic novels. The Laboratory "Artistic Explorations of Ageing and Technology: drawing as elicitation method" explored drawing as a method to examine experiences in social life. Many anthropologists and humanistic researchers also dwell on the role of drawing and its contribution to knowledge production. Such as Afonso and Ramos (2004), Azevedo (2016, 2017), Bonanno (2022), Hendrikson (2008), Ramos (2004), Sherwood González (2022) Taussig (2009, 2011).

to Comics?". He talked about the history of comics, from its beginning to that moment, and presented a sentence that caught our attention and made us reflect on the originality of our work and why comics made it so unique. According to Spiegelman "Comics are time turned into space" (Shao 2014).[7] Thinking about this possibility of transmutation between time and space opens several possible questions to understand these two fundamental categories in the history of Social Sciences. What times and spaces is the author referring to? How can we express the changes in the perception of time and space between our interlocutors? What is the relationship between the notions of presence, time, and space?

We can think of the working time involved in the process of drawing up such a project and turning it into the space of pages. Or, using the very reference of Maus, the time in which that, or those, stories passed converted into spaces on paper. However, what interests us is the existence of the different times – the time needed for production, the moment the author was living, the temporal space in which that story takes place, the time in which the reader finds themselves and is crossed by these stories – being transported and expressed in those small spaces between one panel and another. These gutters are vague spaces of time imagined by the reader. In addition, those stories gain space and materiality that will persist in time. This notion directly dialogues with those workshops we produced to collect reports for the second edition; it became increasingly evident that we needed to think of these materials as documents of their time, as living archives.

In The Class Diary of the Pandemic, we needed to produce the illustrations of each report every week so that the ready-made and published art would also become an invitation to new reports. These dynamics and the limitations imposed by social networks defined some of the aesthetic choices we made in the project. For example, we sought to represent as many elements present in the story as possible in one panel, so it was practically a semiotic exercise to put subtle details that summarized complex ideas of those stories. This was especially true in the first phase of the project, when we designed it to work as posts in our Instagram account (@proeep_unicamp).

When we decided we would dig deeper into the rich material we had in hand and started working on the comic book, the possibilities increased. We could use more frames and formats other than the 1080x1080 pixels of an Instagram post, and we started to create longer dialogues between panels. This last aspect significantly altered the stories we were telling because the relationships between images and words could be expressed in a denser way, and through details we could approach the experiences of subjects.

---

7   The material produced about this Spiegelman presentation is only available on news portals
     like this one: (Shao 05.12.2014) https://www.bostonmagazine.com/arts-entertainment/201
     4/05/12/art-spiegelman-boston-what-happened-to-comics/.

It is precisely through the expressiveness of images and their relationships with the short text excerpts of the reports that readers would be able to apprehend the realities of the Brazilian educational context and its transformations during the pandemic. We chose to work these reports artistically in images because we believe in their communicative power to reveal nuances of social life that are difficult to grasp through written text alone. In speech, only one word can be said at a time, while in images a set of elements can be placed at the same time.

As Sylvia Caiuby Novaes exposes, images have a muted aspect of saying without speaking, inciting comments on what it evokes, without necessarily showing it visually. She points out how, "when the observer allows himself a dip in the image, it evokes and awakens in him feelings, memories and sensations about which he begins to talk" (Novaes 2014, 61).[8]

During the creative process, the production took on greater and greater proportions, and the painting of the panels demanded a lot of time. At some point, we had to decide whether we would make more panels or dedicate ourselves to painting. The choice was not easy; the colors were very important elements to tell those stories. Through them, we were able to create several nuances, such as determining the materials of which objects were made, hair colors and skin tones of characters, or the colors of the sky to circumscribe the moment of the day in which the action took place. Another possible element to represent with colors was the interaction with the lights emitted by electronic equipment, the main, if not the only, means of communication and contact between students and teachers at that time. All these elements need to be reimagined when we start using black and white, after all, these nuances need to be presented in different ways.

Below we present some images of the sketches produced throughout the construction of the two editions to show the elements we have been commenting on, in addition to some other details.

---

8   From the original: "Quando o observador se permite um mergulho na imagem esta evoca e desperta nele sentimentos, lembranças e sensações sobre os quais começa a falar" (Novaes 2014, 61).

Picture 1: Facial expression studies. Drawings by Matheus Fred Schulze.

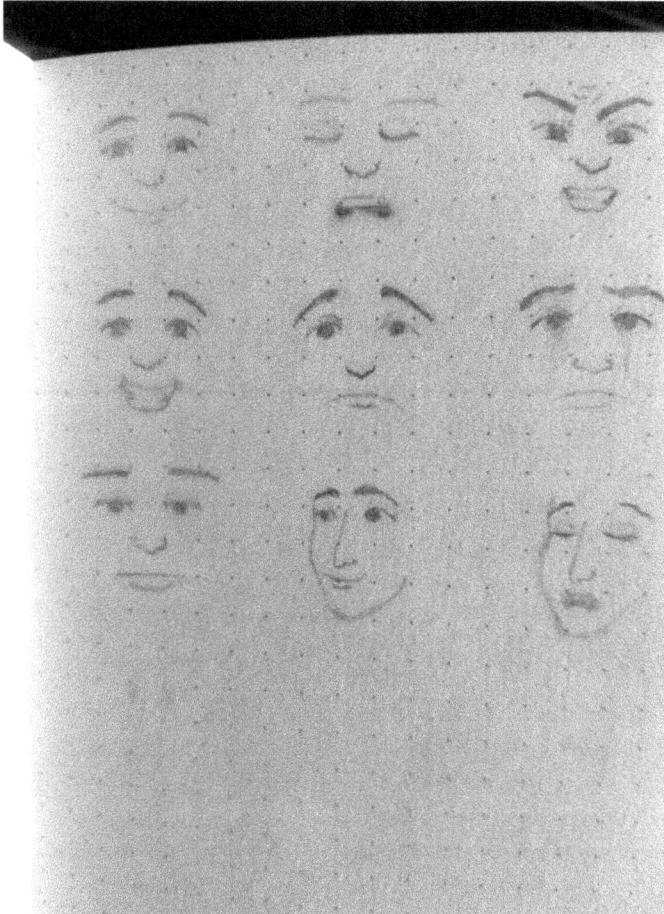

With a limited number of panels and following the previously mentioned logic of concentrating on as much information as possible, the use of facial expressions was essential. The characters needed to be expressive to show the emotions in the stories. In the sketch above, we see an example of facial expression studies that could be used in the reports. The need to use these pantomimes is also related to these new dynamics of presence in a scenario of social isolation. Most reports told a reality of difficult communication between students and teachers, always mediated by virtual spaces and affected by all the adversities to which this medium is subject. So we needed to tell these stories, mostly through moments of silence.

Another interesting element to analyze in the sketches is the way comics were structured.

Picture 2 and 3: Sketches. Drawings by Matheus Fred Schulze.

The picture 2 is a one-page diagram of the first edition of the book. It was the first time of illustrators with this type of work, added to the challenge of adapting the reports to this new format. These aligned factors culminated in a structural choice that caused some problems. For example, some elements were not positioned, such as speech balloons for the drawing of a comic, which created a difficult scenario to work with. The second image shows the structure of a report for the second edition, and it is already possible to perceive the changes that the experience had produced.

Returning to the topic of using specific signs to express complex ideas in the painting, we need to consider that in all this artistic exercise there is the place of the artist. In our work, the choices to express all stories and subtle details present in each one were made by the illustrators. They expressed other people's pandemic experiences using their own experiences during that same period as informant signs for reference on their artistic work. Therefore, from the elements that drew the most attention to stand out in the story to the way one imagines the plan of a house, its furniture, etc., they go through the artist's filter.

Picture 4: "Maria Luiza". Drawings by Matheus Fred Schulze.

For instance, in the report illustrated above, sent by Teacher Maria Luiza, we can see some interesting elements. At one point, she talks about the fact that she used a map, which she had at home, to explain the regions of Brazil and the state of São Paulo – following the proposed syllabus. We then added this element in the background of the space she uses to record her video lessons in the panel. It is not an element directly linked to the story, but through it we can tell she gives lessons that require the use of maps and where this report takes place, as the teacher is in that state.

The stacked books improvising a support for her cell phone was a way to show the precariousness and lack of structure that many teachers had to face. They had to adapt to remote teaching almost without any help from schools and the State. This was, in fact, the technique that the illustrator used when he needed to record some audiovisual material. The blackboard where the educator writes the alphabet is a reference to the fact that she needs to assemble extra content for some students.

In the last panel, we have several details of the report gathered. The computer with internet connection problems while the teacher watches a video provided by the government of São Paulo. This reinforces the locality in which the story is inserted and presents the fact that the teacher is part of in the public education system.

Finally, there is a sticky note on the notebook saying "It is not a lesson!". In her report, Maria Luiza mentions she did not believe that this form of distance learning could be considered teaching. This direct and pertinent criticism of the situation could not be left out of the illustrations, even if briefly. This also informs us about the perceptions about presence, the so precious being together and crucial for pedagogical practice, which completely changed in the new dynamics established by the pandemic.

Picture 5: *"Valéria". Drawings by Matheus Fred Schulze.*

In Valéria's report, we can see other details. In the first panel, a magnifying glass on the cell phone is a narrative resource to show different access difficulties of each individual. Even with the lesson adapted to the online environment, with the use of a presentation, this format may remain inaccessible to some people.

In addition, the position of the comics builds a direct opposition between past and present, clearly showing the differences between these two moments. In person, the dialogue between teacher and students is much easier and more direct. The dynamics and perceptions of physical and online presence is a central point in this section of the report, where the teacher reveals difficulty in establishing connections with her students. Physical distance and access difficulties significantly compromise the teaching and learning process. Showing the opposition between past and present and reinforcing the changes and permanence between these two moments was very important for our work. Through this, we were able to show that realities had changed. Before the pandemic, the classes were synchronous at school, but with social isolation, this synchronicity was not possible for everyone anymore because of a lack of structure, such as a good internet connection and knowledge to use these call platforms, besides common issues that always happens on these virtual spaces. Also, with the pandemic, asynchronous classes were more spread inside educational institutions without training for teachers and students to learn how to deal with this new educational process.

The medium of comics allows us to do this in different ways, enhanced here by the richness of our reports. One of these ways and tools is the positioning of frames within the page. In this case, and several other moments, we used it to present elements, create sensations and intensify others, to tell these stories to our reader.

Finally, we have the issue of lack of structure again, reappearing with some health problems. Beyond the striking representation of bodies and gestures, the proximity between teacher and student to show something in a book is a counterpoint to the online experience with back pain and the need for magnifying glasses. The teacher did not have an adequate space in her home to work remotely, as represented by the use of an unsuitable chair for work, which ended up causing pain in the character.

Picture 6: "Staphanie". Drawings by Matheus Fred Schulze.

In the report above, we can see again the direct opposition between past and present, with the new dynamics experienced by the teacher. Her routine totally changed, as the following panels show. In her report, Stephanie told us she worked many more hours than before. This issue of changing the notion of working time during home office was very present in all reports. We represented it through three panels with colors, indicating morning, afternoon, and evening. This intense work routine sickened the teacher and forced her to change her routine again.

Picture 7 and 8: "Tom". Drawings by Matheus Fred Schulze.

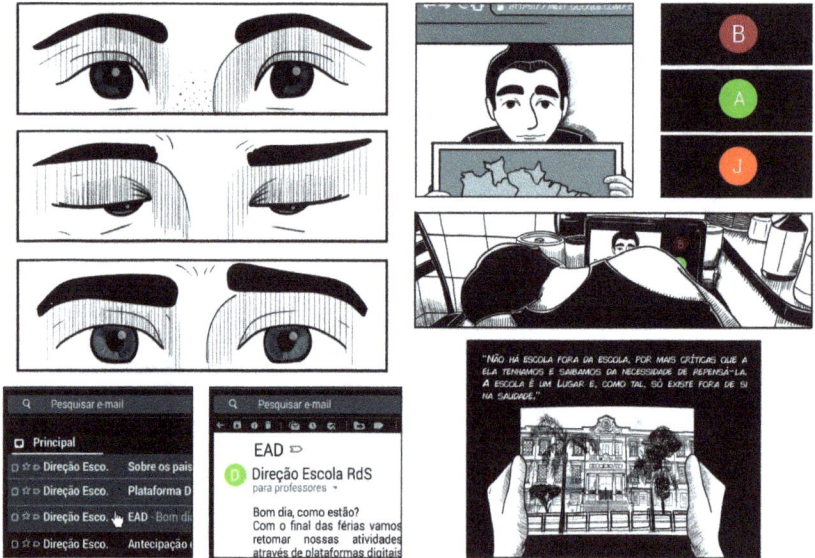

We have Tom's report above. He is a teacher in a private school in the state of São Paulo. In a few lines, he narrated the transition process from face-to-face teaching to remote teaching and all the implications derived from this. Through the images, we can think of different aspects of this process of time/space transformation during the pandemic in teaching and learning environments. These changes go through learning how digital tools work and adapting to being within these spaces. The whole educational practice had to be changed, and this can be seen, for example, in the opposition between the three panels representing the tired and distressed looks in the classroom and the three panels of students with disabled Google Meet cameras.

The transformations and adaptations to the digital presence must also be perceived through bodies, as these phenomena affected all the senses of students and teachers. The senses and feelings of our interlocutors are expressed in the panels in their gestures: the teachers' tired looks, the student propped on the table, and the nostalgia of face-to-face teaching.

Finally, adaptations were not the same for everyone. Not all students had an adequate space for their studies and ended up having their experiences deeply impacted by the lack of structure during remote lessons.

Conclusion

Throughout the development of our work, we were constantly concerned by the experiences of Brazilian students and teachers during the pandemic. Like our interlocutors, we were deeply impressed by the pandemic and its impact on the Brazilian social-political context. The effects of these transformations on the very notion of presence were present in all of us in the most varied ways, expressed in our bodies and our changed perceptions of time and space. Our goal with this work was to bring together this diversity of experiences and express them in a sensitive and intelligible way to a wide audience, promoting conversations and debates about this historical moment and its contemporary developments.

The artistic output of comics to tell stories stands out for enabling the expression of the senses and feelings of those who faced education during the pandemic. This artistic output is a proper anthropological movement, which starts from observation and description towards the details of what connects these stories with what is beyond the particular experiences during the pandemic. Through these reports and our comics, we can see similar senses and emotions shared between teachers and students about the class's environment transformations. Also, how synchronous and asynchronous ways of connecting students and teachers in virtual environments transformed the notion of presence. Our effort is to move out of experience towards expression.

Bibliography

Afonso, Ana Isabel and Manuel João Ramos. 2004. "New Graphics for Old Stories: Representation of local memories through drawings". Pp. 66–83 in Working Images: Visual Research and Representation in Ethnography, edited by A. I. Afonso, L. Kurti e S. Pink. London: Routledge.

Alves, Lise. 2021. "Pandemic puts Brazil back on the world hunger map." *The New Humanitarian*, July 19, 2021. https://www.thenewhumanitarian.org/news-featu re/2021/7/19/pandemic-puts-brazil-back-on-the-world-hunger-map.

Azevedo, Aina. 2016. "Um convite à antropologia desenhada." METAgraphias: met-alinguagem e outras figuras, v. 1 n.1 (1): 194–208.

_____. 2017. "Diário de campo e diário gráfico: contribuições do desenho à antropologia". Altera Revista de Antropologia. v. 2, n. 2.

Bonanno, L. 2022. Of Athens, crises, and other medicines. American Anthropologist, 124(2), 417–425.

Didi-Huberman, Georges. 2016. *Que emoção! Que emoção?* Translated by Cecília Ciscato. São Paulo: Editora 34.

Folman, Ari, David Polonsky and Raquel Zampil. 2017. *O diário de Anne Frank em quadrinhos.* 11th ed. Rio de Janeiro: Record.

Frank, Anne. 1952. *The Diary of a Young Girl.* Translated by B. M. Mooyaart-Doubleday.

Hendrikson, Carol. 2008. "Visual Field Notes: Drawing Insights in the Yucatan". Visual Anthropology Review, 24 (2): 117–132.

Jesus, Carolina Maria De. 1963. *Child of the Dark: the Diary of Carolina Maria de Jesus.* Translated by David St. Clair. New York: Mentor.

Jesus, Carolina Maria De. 2019. *Quarto de despejo.* 10th ed. São Paulo: Ática.

Lino Gomes, Nilma. 2020. "Racismo e novo coronavírus: armas mortíferas no Brasil." *Nexo Jornal*, July 4, 2020. https://www.nexojornal.com.br/ensaio/debate /2020/Racismo-e-novo-coronav%C3%ADrus-armas-mort%C3%ADferas-no-Br asil. London: Valentine Mitchell.

Merleau-Ponty, Maurice. 2004. *Conversas – 1948.* Translated by Fábio Landa and Eva Landa. São Paulo: Martins Fontes.

Novaes, Sylvia Caiuby. 2014. O silêncio eloquente das imagens fotográficas e sua importância na etnografia. *Cadernos de Arte e Antropologia*, 3 (2): 57–67

Pinheiro, João and Sirlene Barbosa. 2021. *Carolina.* 1st ed. São Paulo: Veneta.

Programa de Extensão em Educação Política – UNICAMP. 2020. Diário de Classe da Pandemia. Relatos em Quadrinhos de Professoras sobre a Pandemia de Coronavírus. https://drive.google.com/file/d/1gar2omXHq5Z61Yj2OLEEn4PeV 7-01NM_/view.

Ramírez Ramos, María Fernanda. 2023. "Genocide Of the Yanomami People in Brazil: An Announced Tragedy Involving Bolsonaro." *LatinAmerica Post*, February 2, 2023. https://latinamericanpost.com/43344-genocide-of-the-yanomami-peo ple-in-brazil-an-announced-tragedy-involving-bolsonaro.

Ramos, Manuel João. 2004. "Drawing the lines – The limitation of intercultural ekphrasis." Pp. 147–156 in Working Images: Visual Research and Representation in Ethnography, edited by A. I. Afonso, L. Kurti e S. Pink. London: Routledge.

Rodrigues, Meghie. 2021. "Scientists reel as Brazilian government backtracks on research funds." *Nature*, October 22, 2021. https://www.nature.com/articles/d415 86-021-02886-9.

Shao, Yiquing. 2014. "Art Spiegelman Talks 'What the%@&*! Happened to Comics?'". *Boston Magazine*, May 12, 2014. https://www.bostonmagazine.com/arts-entertai nment/2014/05/12/art-spiegelman-boston-wh at-happened-to-comics/.

Sherwood González, J. 2022. Story of Mirrors: It's Just One of Those Family Stories You Hear. (forthcoming) Studies in Comics 12:1.

Spiegelman, Art. 1986. *Maus: A Survivor's Tale.* New York: Pantheon Books.

_____. 2005. *Maus. Historia Completa*. 1st ed. Translated by Antonio de Macedo Soares. São Paulo: Quadrinhos na Cia.

Taussig, Michael. 2009. "What Do Drawings Want?" Culture, Theory and Critique, vol. 50, issue 2–3: 263–274.

_____. 2011. I swear I saw this. Drawings in fieldwork notebooks, namely my own. Chicago and London: The University of Chicago Press.

GPSR Authorized Representative: Easy Access System Europe, Mustamäe tee
50, 10621 Tallinn, Estonia, gpsr.requests@easproject.com

www.ingramcontent.com/pod-product-compliance
Lightning Source LLC
Chambersburg PA
CBHW070117030426
42335CB00016B/2184